THE FASHION RESOURCE BOOK

Robert Leach

THE FASHION RESOURCE BOOK
RESEARCH FOR DESIGN

With 440 illustrations, 333 in colour

Thames & Hudson

CONTENTS

To Sue McCarthy

Pages 1 & 2 Basso & Brooke Japanese-inspired 'Hi-Tech Romance' collection, Spring/Summer 2009.

First published in the United Kingdom in 2012 by Thames & Hudson Ltd, 181A High Holborn, London WC1V 7QX

The Fashion Resource Book © 2012 Thames & Hudson Ltd, London
Text copyright © 2012 Robert Leach

Designed by Karolina Prymaka
Edited by Kirsty Seymour-Ure

British Library Cataloguing-in-Publication Data
A catalogue record for this book is available from the British Library

ISBN 978-0-500-29035-4

Printed and bound in China by Toppan Leefung Printing Limited

To find out about all our publications, please visit **www.thamesandhudson.com**. There you can subscribe to our e-newsletter, browse or download our current catalogue, and buy any titles that are in print.

FOREWORD

This invaluable book interrogates the notion of research: what it is and how to do it, what it does and why. It directs the reader to a greater understanding of why primary research is fundamental in developing a personal identity as a fashion designer within a global industry.

I have known Robert for more than sixteen years, first as a student, then as an independent designer and later as a fellow educator at Central Saint Martins College of Art and Design in London. Our relationship as a teaching team focused specifically on working with students and their research to encourage them to pursue their own investigative design process enabling them to articulate their own creative voice. Robert's extensive knowledge of clothing history, details and cut is unparalleled and is evidenced through his hands-on study of fashion practice, as both a trained designer and an innovative pattern cutter.

One key collaboration was an annual tailoring project held at Central Saint Martins for second-year students. Its basis was to assist students in understanding the expansive possibilities of what tailoring could be, and it was underpinned by a 'creative briefing' process and supported by Robert's vast knowledge of the subject. Its resulting success was the binding of the design process and the construction research process of the garment, and the understanding that the two methods are inseparable.

Below Porters carrying trunks on their backs in the traditional manner, in early 20th-century La Paz, Bolivia. Photograph by Frank G. Carpenter.

Opposite The John Galliano Autumn/ Winter 2004 collection, featuring luggage carried in a similar manner.

What sets this book apart is the breathtaking knowledge conveyed through the personal insights of the professionals involved. The eclectic mix of visuals with supporting interviews by real design professionals from within education and industry serves to provide a consistent message – that of 'the personal'.

The interviews uncover some of the often veiled or presumptive ideas of the way in which research occurs. This process can come only from those who do it and who know it instinctively. Reading through these illuminating case studies we see articulated the continual need for primary research, as evidenced by the traceable threads of the personal design identities involved.

As a self-employed fashion designer working within my own business structure and crafting my own vision throughout, I feel it important to note that my work was always grounded in a strong and substantive research base. I have always believed in the pursuit of innovative methods of fabric development for structuring a personal design identity from within what is a very congested industry.

From the very early beginnings of my career, the nature of my work and the research involved attracted attention not only from the fashion industry but also from international curators and other creative practitioners with whom I collaborated on many projects. It was often acknowledged that my work could be interpreted in the context of 'designer as researcher'.

One key collection was the 'Braille Collection' launched in 1998, researched through interviews with the Royal National Institute for the Blind. Relatively ignored at the time, this collection went on to be exhibited globally, utilized by the design team of Renault Cars and featured in the major retrospective exhibition 'Archaeology of the Future: 20 years of Trend Forecasting' in 2009 by the world's most renowned trend forecaster, Li Edelkoort.

It is so important for students and designers to understand that they cannot design alone in the world. This book helps to disseminate that information and bring an openness to all creative thinking. Research develops a personal memory bank of grounded critical thinking, enabling a designer to facilitate sustainable outcomes within a global fashion industry that is often running to catch up with itself.

Shelley Fox
Donna Karan Professor of Fashion
Parsons The New School for Design, New York

INTRODUCTION

In modern fashion design and education, the ability to carry out thorough visual research is considered a key skill; without it design cannot exist. No designer can create in a vacuum; the creative mind needs constant food and stimulus. The world today is obsessed with newness and innovation. In a sphere where you will hear that 'everything has been done before', it is the vital role of research to move the design process on, to create new inspirations and to bring new ideas together. Without solid research there can be no new design.

Above Coco Chanel wearing one of her signature tweed two-piece suits.

Opposite A young Yves Saint Laurent sketching on a chalkboard.

Alexander McQueen, one of the greats
of late 20th-century fashion.

The world of fashion design has changed enormously over the past hundred or so years. Even the concept of the 'fashion designer' is relatively new, being unknown until the early twentieth century, before which there were only dressmakers and tailors, and then the great French couturiers.

The early couturiers made seasonal variations of popular dress, but it was not until the time of the First World War that designers as we know them today came into being.

French designer Coco Chanel was perhaps the earliest and the most influential. The 'flapper' style of the 1920s was mostly her invention, and she championed the little black dress, womenswear inspired by menswear, the Chanel suit, matelot style and costume jewelry. She was also probably the first designer to use the logo, her intertwined Cs as recognizable today as they were eighty years ago.

In the late 1920s another female designer emerged in Paris. A friend of the great artists of the day, including Marcel Duchamp, Jean Cocteau and Man Ray, Elsa Schiaparelli began her business by producing a collection of trompe l'oeil sweaters very much in the Surrealist manner. Much of her design was inspired by art, and was, indeed, themed: she was truly one of the first designers to be inspired by what was happening around her, and by things outside fashion, rather than just by clothing itself. Referred to by Chanel, rather disparagingly, as 'the Italian artist who makes clothes', Schiaparelli flourished until the Second World War. Like Chanel, she leaves behind an enduring fashion legacy.

After the war had ended in 1945, Christian Dior came to the fore with his 'New Look', a much softer and more voluminous style than the austere, boxy look of wartime. Fashion again became a business of subtle reinvention, with little informing it other than the clothes themselves – until the arrival on the fashion scene of the young designer Yves Saint Laurent. Saint Laurent was employed by Christian Dior, and on Dior's untimely death in 1957, he became the head of the House of Dior. After mixed reviews at Dior and a spell of National Service, he founded the House of Saint Laurent, and set about the business of creating fashion trends like no one before him. The Beatnik style, the graphic grid paintings of Mondrian, the colours of North Africa, the reinvention of the tuxedo for women, the gypsy look and the safari suit... all were employed to great effect. His subsequent invention of prêt-à-porter, or ready-to-wear, made fashion younger, more accessible and, most of all, more fun.

Art and fashion, as in the 1920s and 1930s, again became bedfellows with the advent of Op art and Pop art in the 1950s–60s; fashion was moving very much more quickly, and designers began to be inspired by the fast-moving world around them, as well as beginning to look back in time for fresh inspiration. New innovations in fabrics and manufacturing added to the momentum, combined with the new disposable income of the young and their increasing interest in fashion.

1
THE RESEARCH PROCESS

Designers take inspiration from many sources, and there are countless possible uses and outcomes of visual research. In this section, designers, students and companies are discussed from the point of view of their research. In some cases examples of research material have been provided by the designer or company in question, while in other cases imagery is provided as a 'visual review' of a given collection or look, as well as sketchbooks and mood board work from designers and from students on the world's top fashion courses.

Examples of the use of research provide just one point of view; there are always many possible outcomes, even from one single image – it is the way a designer taps into their own personal aesthetic that makes the outcome uniquely their own. Each designer has a signature, their unique handwriting: it is this that sets them apart. Each will approach their research in a different way; for some it might be about clothing, for others a period in time, a character (real or fictional), a colour, a narrative or a mood, perhaps involving found images, photographs, sculpture or architecture. Some designers, such as John Galliano and Vivienne Westwood, excel at mixing up historical periods or in bringing different areas of research together. Galliano's 'Honcho Woman', for example, presented in March 1996, was an unlikely melding of the Duchess of Windsor style with that of the Native American. Other designers might specialize in clothes-based research, such as the reinventions of specific clothing types, especially those rooted in a brand's history. For example, the trench coat is reworked seasonally at Burberry by Christopher Bailey and the design team; Levi's reinvents its jeans, often based on the company's heritage; and Karl Lagerfeld adapts and reworks the Chanel suit and associated signatures at the House of Chanel. Cultural references and research, gained perhaps through travel or museum visits, might inspire silhouette, colour or type of fabric, while some approaches are altogether more esoteric, with various designers being inspired by much more abstract concepts, such as movement at Lanvin, reappropriation at Maison Martin Margiela or the distortion of the human form at Comme des Garçons.

Willie Walters, course director of the fashion BA at Central Saint Martins, writes: 'We used to be asked why we don't do history of costume lectures, but we feel that's so narrow, and while it's important for students to know about the history of costume, it's vital that their research bases encompass the possibilities of, say, a flower, or maybe a bathroom floor, as inspiration. We start here with a white project, which is very open: they might be designing a suit, or a tent, or one a strange blob: the idea of that is to get them researching and excited about their first project. One student in the final year was inspired by a form of dancing from Soweto called Street Party; they're wearing almost western clothes but tied over with big skirts, in an African style, wrapped garments, doing amazing dances. The final result looked much more English, him being

Colonel St John, of the Queen's Own
Oxfordshire Hussars, leaving St James's
Palace, London, 1925.

an English boy. If we were all given the same set of research, we'd all come up with very different things and that's what keeps it interesting.'

Shelley Fox, Donna Karan Professor of Fashion and course leader of MFA studies at Parsons The New School for Design, New York, asserts: 'There should always be a personal reason for design; it should come from looking at the world around you and really seeing it. Research and experimentation don't necessarily make it into a design in a literal way, but they are part of the process of investigating, understanding context, and questioning what you are doing and why you are doing it. We want to encourage students to develop their creativity, but also provide them with a reality check; ultimately, a design has to hold up on its own and prove viable in the world.'

Fashion awareness is another key area for the designer – not only a knowledge of the history of fashion and clothing, but also an acute awareness of current trends, the collective themes that run across collections and are identified by journalists and forecasters. These identifiable trends are very much seen as the driving force of fashion. Alongside trend awareness, all designers should absorb the zeitgeist; art, literature, popular culture and products, architecture, electronics and interior design – all can be seen to influence contemporary fashion, and vice versa.

Andrew Ibi, designer, lecturer and owner of designer womenswear boutique The Convenience Store in London, says: 'The best places for inspiration are always staring you right in the face and are personal and first-hand. My work is always based on looking at these signs and pointers and appropriating them back into our culture. But it has to make sense to you. I've spent three years in a shop window watching the world go by and it's giving me a true and honest reflection of my community. It's like a panoramic viewpoint, nothing gets past me and nothing is lost.'

'My research work,' Ibi says, 'will always revolve around the present and contemporary and will usually involve identity and culture. My design work is quite autobiographical and challenges these ideas fully, mixing identity, age, gender, culture and social standing. London in 2011 is an incredibly complex and ever-evolving place, at every turn it throws new dynamics all around us. It is down to me to find the correct interpretation of this communication. Some of these ideas are translating into physical spaces of interaction and experiment; the research ingredients are made up of very modern and forward-thinking observations and responses. Perhaps we are finding new ways of feeding our observations back to the observed?'

Also on the subject of visual research, from an academic perspective, Elinor Renfrew, course director of the fashion BA at Kingston University, London, feels: 'Inspiration can be found anywhere and everywhere – if we were to give a list then the students wouldn't look beyond that list. For me it's always the places I haven't thought of; museums and galleries, costume, art, film, photography, book fairs, and other places that we haven't known or heard about. Often a particular book becomes key for research at a given time and many students pick up on the same book, but in that respect, a hundred times worse is the Internet. It's far too secondary as a research base, everyone downloads the same imagery – students need to get out into the world, seek out the new.'

Willie Walters goes on to say: 'In my nineteen years at Central Saint Martins I've seen so many different areas of research, and have delighted in seeing the variety over the years. Every year new things turn up and I think to myself how amazing that new ideas are continuing to happen. I saw one student who missed his friends back in Liverpool, so he got images of his friends, one of whom wore glasses, and he created the shape of these glasses, and I was thinking to myself, "how on earth is this ever going to be some sort of garment?" – but he created something wonderful from that. There's a final-year girl from China who based her collection on the disappearing streets of old Beijing: they're all but gone now, it's very sad. She is Chinese and mourning the loss of her heritage and culture.'

It is clear that the overriding consensus of industry professionals, both designers and educators, is not only that research is an absolutely vital tool, but that inspiration is everywhere and in everything: one just needs to learn how to find it and best employ it. It is up to individuals to bring their particular take on it, to utilize it, and to create from it.

Alexander McQueen Autumn/Winter
2008 Hussar-inspired jacket over
voile dress.

MAISON MARTIN MARGIELA

Founded in 1988 and based in Paris, Maison Martin Margiela was the brainchild of Belgian designer Martin Margiela. Since its founding the company has pushed the accepted boundaries of fashion design, whether it be in its casting of models of all ages, its remaking of 'found' garments, known as Replicas, its recycling of garments and fabrics, or its staff collective comprising sixteen different nationalities of designers. The anonymity of Martin Margiela himself is a deliberate comment on the celebrity cult of the fashion designer. The team is quoted as saying that 'the only thing we wish to push to the forefront is our fashion'.

From the outset, the company favoured white as a signature colour: offices, boutiques, showrooms and exhibitions have all been painted in particular shades of white. Several key themes have emerged during its twenty-year history, each uniquely the company's own, some of which have since filtered into the mainstream.

In the 'Doll's Wardrobe' collection of Spring/Summer 1995, dolls' garments were reproduced at human scale, disproportionate details and manufacture being faithfully reproduced; large fastenings and stitch sizes gave the garments a surreal air.

In the Spring/Summer 1996 'Trompe L'Oeil' collection, photographs of more complex garments were printed on to garments of much simpler construction – a 1920s beaded evening gown on a T-shirt dress, for example, or the inside of a dress of complicated structure on the outside of a simple shift.

For Spring/Summer 1998 Maison Martin Margiela produced the 'Flat' collection of garments constructed in such a way that they would fall completely flat if dropped; shoulders

Opposite and below **Images from the Maison Martin Margiela retrospective celebrating Margiela's 20th anniversary at the MOMU fashion museum in Antwerp, Belgium, in 2008–9.**

were displaced or zips inserted so the garment could be unzipped to lie flat, in what was, in fact, the antithesis of tailoring.

Oversized clothing has also been a key theme over many of the designer's collections, none more so than Spring/Summer 2000, when each garment in the collection was first made regular sized in white cotton, then scaled up to a size 74 in a variety of fabrics.

In 2003 Maison Martin Margiela started the manufacture of 'Replicas', faithful copies of found garments. Each is given a label describing the type of garment and its provenance and history; for example, a jacket might be labelled and described as 'Boy's tailored jacket, France, 1970'.

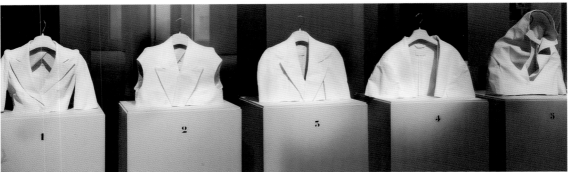

PAUL SMITH   Paul Smith, born in Nottingham in 1946, is one of the most successful British fashion designers of all time. He started his – still independently owned – business in 1970, at first selling the clothes of such designers as Margaret Howell and Kenzo. He then moved on to designing and producing his own classic designs with a very British edge, which have become loved the world over. In 1976, he became one of the first retailers to inhabit the then deserted Covent Garden area of London, a former fruit and vegetable market that is now internationally renowned for its fashion stores and is very much a tourist destination. That same year he showed his menswear collection in Paris for the first time.

Smith's quirky sense of humour and mischief and his ability to mix the modern and the traditional have propelled him to fashion stardom worldwide. Paul Smith clothing is sold in seventy-five countries, including stores in London, Nottingham, Paris, Milan, New York, Hong Kong, Singapore, Taiwan, the Philippines, Korea, Kuwait and the UAE; there are more than two hundred stores in Japan alone.

Smith travels extensively and is a keen photographer, recording and collecting inspirational things to fuel both his own imagination and that of his design team. The shops themselves also very much reflect the character of the man and his designs – a quintessential Britishness peppered with quirky and surprising elements. The shops house not only Paul Smith clothing but also jewelry, books, art, antiques and an array of interesting and beautiful products. The work of other British designers will often be showcased alongside Smith's personal collections of art and curios.

Paul Smith explains his eclectic aesthetic thus: 'We're a leading and uniquely British brand. We mix up one-off antiques with high-quality tailoring: the chair you sit on when you buy a suit is for sale and we can wrap the suit and have the chair waiting for you when you get home.'

'I am fascinated that whatever you pick up has been designed with a particular purpose in mind, whether it's grand or silly. This means that almost anything can serve as a visual prompt. A Chinese cigarette packet might suggest a new way to pack socks. A naff piece of fabric from a market in Egypt might make me think of a loud shirt that might look great under a cashmere suit. An Indian dancing doll, which someone has just plonked on a smart book, could spark an idea of juxtaposing kitsch with posh, rough with smooth, bright with bold, pattern on pattern.'

Portrait of Paul Smith in his workspace surrounded by inspirational items.

Top and inset **Light stream image by Paul Smith, subsequently digitized and printed onto a silk scarf.**

Left **Paul Smith's menswear on the catwalk, in a collection inspired by the fabrics, prints and colours of the textiles worn by women in India.**

Above **Women in brightly coloured traditional dress carrying water from a well outside Pushkar, India.**

Opposite and left **Photographs by Paul Smith of the vintage American cars that are found all over the island of Cuba.**

Above **The images have then been translated into digital prints to adorn silk scarves.**

ANNA SUI

American womenswear designer Anna Sui was born in Detroit in 1964 and studied at Parsons The New School For Design in New York. In 1991 she opened her store 113 Greene Street in the Soho area of New York. The store, with its lavender walls, black antique furnishings and dolls' heads, would come to embody the signature style of the Anna Sui brand. In her 'think space' above her present store in New York's Manhattan, she surrounds herself with objects she finds inspirational; she describes the room as her three-dimensional mood board. She is particularly fond of the black-and-white painted pottery designs of Danish painter and ceramicist Bjorn Wiinblad, and his influence can be clearly seen in the monochrome multi-scale patterned border prints on her charmingly whimsical dresses.

Below Anna Sui in what she describes as her 'think space' – her inspirational environment.

Below right Elements of Anna Sui's collection of 20th-century black-and-white ceramics.

Opposite left Bjorn Wiinblad design (c. 1960) on ceramic plaque for Nymolle.

Opposite right Dress inspired by 20th-century Scandinavian ceramic designs from Anna Sui's Spring/Summer 2011 collection.

STEPHEN JONES   Saint Martins-trained milliner Stephen Jones opened his first shop in London's Covent Garden in 1980 and soon became the milliner of choice for rock stars and royalty alike, his whimsical, playful and exquisitely crafted designs always capturing the fashion mood of the moment. Jones has collaborated with numerous international designers during the course of his career, from Rei Kawakubo and Jean Paul Gaultier through to his spectacular work for Dior with John Galliano.

Stephen Jones's work is represented in museums around the world and was recently the subject of a touring exhibition that began at London's Victoria and Albert Museum before moving on to Belgium's fashion museum in Antwerp, MOMU.

The hats featured here are from the Summer 2011 'Drifting and Dreaming' collection.

'I think there is not a moment in the day when I am not inspired, as at this stage in life I have realized my work is autobiographical. Therefore the connection between experience and turning it into a hat must be as direct and fluid as possible. The more it is studied the worse it becomes; my consciousness merely gets in the way… The best hats are created on the whim of the moment, their spontaneity refreshing me and the wearer.'

Delicate, dreamy hats made by Stephen
Jones, inspired by images of the
natural world: the seashore (opposite)
and the evening sky (this page).

STUDIO M Since setting up its design studio twenty years ago in Bermondsey in southeast London, the original Studio M Design Consultancy has developed to include M Lab and M Marketing, offering a full creative service to the fashion industry. The founding members, all previously from senior design positions at high-profile international fashion companies, have a clear idea of the services that can be offered by a small independent specialist creative team to support larger corporate and mid-size companies. Such services include analysis of colour trends and style trends, product assessments, concepts, print and textile design and full design packages.

The ethics of the studio have remained the same since it was established, providing as it does an absolute bespoke service and respecting confidentiality in this competitive industry. Clients are treated wholly as individuals, with specific brand or trend concepts tailor-made to their requirements. This level of brand awareness requires great creative research skills and a passion for the industry.

A talented small in-house team works with specialist freelancers and young fashion graduates to produce individual concepts suited to the specific needs of the client.

Solid original research, together with a heavy dose of instinct, form the basis to all Studio M's client projects. This is complemented by the use of information from M Lab, which gives the studio its own vision of forthcoming colour trends and is not restricted by specific client requirements.

Original research is constant at the studio, with designers making regular visits to international art exhibitions, vintage markets, graduate shows, book launches, design lectures and fairs – or simply style-spotting and people-watching in the streets. The trend antenna is highly tuned so that emerging ideas, colours and concepts are instinctively spotted. Additional specific trend research time is allocated at the beginning of each season, when designers choose where and how they want to research the seasonal trends. Individual ideas are researched in preparation for a big design brainstorm to decide the direction the season will take.

Many fashion companies do not have the resources for this kind of specialist research and knowledge, and many a good designer of product does not have the time and resources to stop and produce the level of trend and colour presentation required up to six or more times a year. For Studio M's designers, the research bug does not stop even on holidays or at weekends, so ingrained is it into the designer's psychic DNA. A curious mind and a quest for knowledge are intrinsic, as is the ability to edit clearly and focus on the true elements that will make a new fashion or textile trend.

Below and opposite **Garment archive documentary images by Studio M and colour box images for client presentation.**

MARIA CORNEJO

In conversation, the Chilean-born, British-trained and New York-based designer Maria Cornejo asserted that she is not the sort of designer who starts from a traditionally themed point of view, but is more likely to take a deeply personal or cerebral approach to her designing for her Maria Cornejo + Zero brand. She is not, for example, inspired by vintage clothing, but rather will take inspiration from her feelings and emotions, from her travels – to Greece, India or Turkey – and from the personal photographs she snaps on her iPhone along the way, some of which have found their way into her collections as digital prints.

Cornejo loves the concept of nature reclaiming its rightful place in the world, taking over again, after being pushed out by mankind for so long; the way in which, against the odds, a wildflower can seed itself in the crack of a wall and flourish. She was inspired to create her Spring/Summer 2010 collection after reading Alan Weisman's speculative science book *The World Without Us* (2007), which imagines in great detail a scenario whereby humanity disappears and nature reclaims the earth. Based on four elements – urban white noise, grass, wood and water – the collection began with white, strong, architectural pieces of geometric cut, then, as the show progressed, the pieces gradually softened in silhouette and form. Travelling through those elements, the garments in the collection became softer, cut as they were from circular shapes, and more naturalistic; fabrics moved and draped more, alluding to the feeling that nature had indeed reclaimed its place and triumphed.

Maria Cornejo cites her fashion idols as being Madeleine Vionnet and Madame Grès, both masters of the same cut and drape technique that she herself employs, in what was then the male-dominated world of the early twentieth century.

Above **Portrait of Maria Cornejo.**

Opposite **Maria Cornejo Spring/Summer 2010 catwalk images featuring the four concepts she used as inspiration (clockwise from top left); urban white noise, water, grass and wood.**

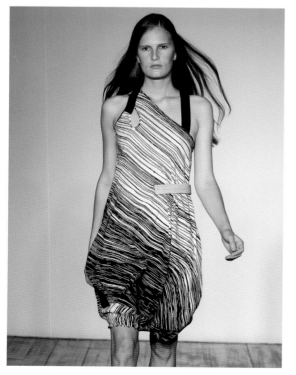

HAND & LOCK

Hand & Lock are bespoke embroiderers to the fashion industry, the theatre, the armed forces and the Church. The company holds a significant historical archive of embroidery samples and patterns, stored in rooms above its workshops, which are regularly drawn on for contemporary commissions. These historic patterns are archived according to geography, ethnicity, branch of the armed forces, religion and all manner of other classifications.

The company's roots are very much older than one might imagine. In 1767 gold-lacemen called Hand, originally Huguenot (French Protestant) refugees from Flanders, set themselves up in London, probably in Spitalfields, where many Huguenots settled and which was a centre of the silk-weaving industry. Gold-lace-making had originally been an Italian skill, which the Hands learned and perfected. Garments trimmed with gold lace and embroidery were a measure of status at this time, with heraldic art indicating the wearer's rank, distinction and achievements. The Hand company flourished as military embroiderers.

In London in 1956, a young designer named Stanley Lock took over the running of the well-established C.E. Phipps embroidery business, which had been founded in 1898, and renamed the company S. Lock Ltd. Over the following half century it reached new heights, working with such renowned couturiers as Christian Dior, Norman Hartnell and Hardy Amies. Lock earned a Royal Warrant, and royal commissions included gowns for the Queen, the Queen Mother, Princess Anne and Princess Diana. The company's extravagant embroidery and beading were used in numerous stage productions, musicals and films.

In 2001 the two companies, S. Lock and M. Hand, merged to form Hand & Lock; two years later it joined with MBA Costumes. All the elements of military, fashion and couture, and entertainment were thereby brought together under one roof in London's West End, and the Hand & Lock brand was created. The companies' respective archive material was consolidated to form a valuable resource for the future.

Above **The Hand & Lock coat of arms.**

Opposite top **Some of the historical embroidery patterns in Hand & Lock's archive.**

Opposite bottom **A worker embroidering an ecclesiastical piece at Hand & Lock.**

BASSO & BROOKE

Bruno Basso and Chris Brooke's inspiration for Spring/Summer 2009 was the idea of a 'High-Tech Romance'. Following a research trip to the Far East for inspirational stimulus, the design duo immersed themselves in a Japanese, rather well-organized urban chaos. Drenched in luminous refinement, the collection reflected a positive and optimistic lifestyle expressed through colour and a love of nature.

The story offered a glimpse into the spirit and grandeur of Japan's Heian era, a classical age of art and literature when fine art, poetry and music were considered the most important social attributes. 'We were inspired by the Japanese notion of flow, the laws and metrics of their aesthetic,' enthuse the designers, who took from the Orient a sophisticated language that reveres both the beauty of nature and the power of technology. Fusing nature and future, they responded to the contrasts of Japan that they experienced. As the original pioneers of digital print in fashion, the team pushed textile technology still further by laser cutting and seamlessly bonding new fabric combinations on to their signature prints.

The asymmetrical essence of natural elements was an important influence for this collection's prints. Traditional Japanese motifs, including rabbits, birds, flowers, waves, sumi-e strokes (ink-wash painting) and calligraphy, are celebrated and contrasted against simple and technological graphic patterns. The blurred rush of lights that the designers witnessed while driving through Tokyo at night informs strong colours – coral red, iris blue, intense black. Sunny early mornings in the gardens of Kyoto bring us celestial blues, pale roses, salmons and hyper-real pastels.

Signature dresses were the foundation of the collection, with the technical construction of the garments being mathematical and logical. A dress inspired by a basket weave was cut in one piece and intricately pin-tucked to create three-dimensional shapes; external tucking created an abstract drapery in silk jersey; and in contrast duchesse satin was folded graphically to create an updated hourglass silhouette.

Master milliner Stephen Jones (see pages 26–27) created oversized kirby grips and hairpins, a simple but strikingly beautiful addition. The application of Swarovski crystals added another dimension, which sparkles luminously over delicate georgette dresses. Raouda Assaf collaborated with the couple, producing sculptural shoes that evoked both the streamlined shape of the future and the softness of nature.

Opposite top and above right Images from the Basso & Brooke Spring/Summer 2009 'High-Tech Romance' Japanese-inspired collection.

Opposite left Light-stream images taken by the pair in Tokyo on their research trip.

Opposite right A digital print from the collection featuring Japanese motifs.

Above A Japanese woman wearing a kimono and holding a parasol.

HANNAH MARSHALL

Hannah Marshall's aesthetic is one of luxury minimalism, in the form of strong silhouettes that empower women. The concepts behind her work involve identity, privacy and control, her main areas of research including uniformity, clones, gender, sensuality, transformation, armour, exposure, voyeurism, secret messages, and more. Other areas of her research are led by technology and innovations and what lies between humans and our increasingly digital world. Another strong force behind her work is music; she believes words and sounds can capture something that communicates to people on different levels.

According to Marshall, 'The Hannah Marshall woman is strong and uncompromising with a sense of confidence; she isn't any particular age or type of person; it is a certain attitude and aesthetic that is shared no matter what part of the globe she is in and what she does. In terms of style and persona my icons are diverse but equally unapologetic and respected – Tilda Swinton, Grace Jones, Carmen Dell'Orefice, Kristen McMenamy, Björk, Alison Mosshart, Siouxsie Sioux and Patti Smith.

'My brand also has quite a musical following, including Florence Welch of Florence and the Machine, Rihanna, Natasha Khan (Bat For Lashes), Alison Mosshart (The Kills), Blondie, Skin (Skunk Anansie), Beth Ditto (Gossip), Lady Gaga and Jessie J. My most exciting moment has to be seeing the iconic cover of *Wonderland* magazine with the incredible Janet Jackson wearing my Spine Sleeve Dress, which was custom-made especially for her. I am a huge fan of all musicians with the surname Jackson, so I am very proud of this.

'I have dressed Florence and the Machine for performances, photo shoots and videos but I think the most exciting time for me was creating a custom-designed leather, chiffon and Swarovski crystal bodysuit that she wore in the "Drumming" video directed by the legendary Dawn Shadforth and styled by Aldene Johnson. I love creating special pieces for artists such as Florence, since not only do they come to life and give the piece a heartbeat, but my work is digitally immortalized.

'In a world flooded with clones, clothing is the single most powerful language to create our own physical identity. It is important to be ourselves and wear on our bodies what represents us, or what message we want to convey to the world. I design clothes to empower women, strong silhouettes made from contrasting, tactile fabrications that both conceal and reveal the body in ways that make a woman feel confident.'

The imagery we see here on Hannah Marshall's studio wall is from the Autumn/Winter 2010 'Army

Below **Hannah Marshall photographed against her mood wall.**

Opposite **Hannah Marshall's studio,** showing the striking black-and-white imagery used for inspiration and research.

of Me' collection. She was heavily inspired by music, and her wall includes many iconic images of singer Grace Jones and the incredible imagery that came out of Jones's collaboration with the legendary art director Jean-Paul Goude in the late 1970s. The concept behind the 'Army of Me' collection was body modification and self-empowerment, leading to a series of powerful silhouettes that create a chapter of the Hannah Marshall story. Goude's pioneering, and at that time unorthodox, approach to photographic manipulation, coupled with the sleek, androgynous persona of Grace Jones, is at the very core of the collection's direction.

STYLESIGHT

Stylesight is a leading online provider of trend content, tools and technology for creative professionals in the fashion and style industries. Founded in 2003 by apparel-manufacturing veteran Frank Bober, Stylesight targets style professionals involved in the creative design and product development processes, who can use the content and tools built in to its 'Creative Platform' to make the design journey faster, more efficient and more accurate. Stylesight is based in New York, London, Hong Kong and Shanghai, with additional offices in style capitals around the globe.

As senior vice president of trend analysis, Sharon Graubard expands upon Stylesight's fresh concept of trend analysis for every major market. Directing the New York headquarters' continual supply of unique content, she works closely with the editorial staff to create informative trend analysis for Stylesight's global subscribers. Her ability accurately to pinpoint and predict shifts in colour and silhouette through a larger analysis of street, runway and culture supports the company's ability to detect, interpret and transmit the global impulses of the style industry.

When asked which designers are currently utilizing research in an exciting way, Sharon said: 'Miuccia Prada might seem like an obvious choice, but she is outstanding in taking inspiration from all sorts of sources and spinning avant-garde collections that also somehow resonate with a wide range of customers and become aspiration pieces. She may use fairy-tale illustrations one season, and Elvis Presley another, but always comes up with something compelling and original. Consuelo Castiglioni for Marni is another designer whose research shows in her vintage home furnishings fabrics, in her mid-century modern shapes, and in her artist collaborations (she used artist Gary Hume for T-shirt graphics last spring). Dries Van Noten uses ethnic textiles in surprising new ways that both celebrate the original and push them into new territory. The Rodarte sisters are inspired by all sorts of things – a drive through Texas where they observed factory workers on their way to work in the early dawn. Yohji Yamamoto researches historical clothing beautifully, as does Vivienne Westwood, both making time-honoured styles absolutely relevant and wearable for today.'

Regarding key areas of research she states: 'The runways are invaluable. Watching key, innovative designers and analysing what they choose to show each season, and how they put it all together, is very inspiring. Often it is a collection that at first appears repellent that offers the most inspiration. It is worthwhile contemplating the collections and "cracking the code"

Below **Web spread of Trend and Colour Forecast from stylesight.com.**

Opposite **'Stylesightings' – straight-up images of street style, an endless source of inspiration.**

each season. But for designers everything is research: people at a party, kids on their way to school, film, art, et cetera. It's important to be artistically inspired but it's also important to understand a particular market, and for that, retailers, magazines and blogs are important touchpoints.

'Lastly, it is essential to use oneself as research; to pull a vision directly out of your own taste, aesthetics, and desires. Not necessarily to be idiosyncratic, but to offer a true vision to the world: even if you are charged with designing a generic product for a mass-market brand, make sure your approach is authentic and truly felt. The customer, who is the end-user, will feel it too.'

REI KAWAKUBO   Rei Kawakubo founded Comme des Garçons in 1969, but it was not until 1981 that she held her first show in Paris; her monochrome, asymmetrical offerings, ripped, torn and with unfinished hems, caused a storm. Western fashion had seen nothing like it before. These ideas have, in some cases, taken decades to filter through to the mass market, but they are undoubtedly there, and unquestionably belong to Rei Kawakubo. She also borrowed from the punk aesthetic of the late 1970s, colouring it black and giving the look a much more intellectual and esoteric air, never more famously than in her knitted sweaters with holes, here described by France Grand in her 1998 book *Comme des Garçons*:

'The famous black pullover with holes in it, often taken for the black flag of anarchy, suggests elegance of a different sort: the confidence of dancers exercising, the photographs of Marilyn Monroe in her sweater, of Jack Kerouac on the road, Pollock in his studio, modern jazz, Living Theatre, the films of Jean-Luc Godard, everything that loosens the rigid nuts and bolts in the machinery of received ideas.'

Seminal collections since have included 'Body Becomes Dress' in 1997, a radical offering of clothing with padded lumps and bumps in unconventional places, mostly removable, but ground-breaking and shocking for the fashion establishment in the way it challenged established perceptions of beauty and the female form.

In 2004 Rei Kawakubo opened a London store, Dover Street Market. Situated near chic Bond Street, the shop stocks not only Comme des Garçons clothing but also ranges from other designers whom Kawakubo invites to share their creative vision within her space; the selected designers often create exclusive lines and displays for Dover Street Market.

Comme des Garçons has also, over the years, collaborated with many other brands, including Levi Strauss, Converse, Nike, Cutler and Gross, Lacoste, Speedo, Fred Perry and Louis Vuitton, while towards the end of 2008 the company joined forces with H&M and brought a range of Comme des Garçons clothing to the high street.

The company's advertising imagery is always instantly recognizable and thought-provoking, comprising images of clothes alongside photography, portraits and anything Rei Kawakubo finds beautiful or inspiring at the time; they are often the result of an artistic collaboration. Artists involved have included Gilbert & George, Mondongo, the Quay Brothers, Chinese artist Ai Weiwei, photographer Cindy Sherman and choreographer Merce Cunningham.

Opposite **Interior view of Dover Street Market, designed by Rei Kawakubo.**

Left **Comme des Garçons Autumn/ Winter 2011.**

2
RESEARCH AND INSPIRATION

HISTORICAL RESEARCH

Designers constantly look back to the past for inspiration: a portrait by an old master, the drapery on an ancient Greek statue, flappers from the 1920s, Regency dandies – these are all grist to the designer's mill.

The history of fashion and clothing is the designer's largest resource, and it is important for the student to have a sound working knowledge of all that has come before. All designers, whatever their particular discipline, draw on the past as well as using their own skills, experiences and vision to create for the future.

There are many designers currently drawing overtly on this rich historical past, each in a distinctive way. John Galliano is fashion's maestro of historical adaptation, succeeding in combining fashion elements of, say, the 1920s with those of the 1960s. While remaining recognizable to anyone with a knowledge of fashion history, in his hands they become something new and beautiful, and completely his own; he moves through the decades with a masterly hand. In contrast, Marc Jacobs is fast becoming the master of twentieth-century Americana in fashion design, his work differing from the 'heritage' style of Ralph Lauren's in that typically American themes from different periods in the country's history – the depression, the 1950s, military uniform – are all thrown into his own particular stylistic melting pot, often alongside film and cultural references, to great effect.

The late Alexander McQueen also drew regularly on historical themes and concepts for his collections. The early 'Highland Rape' collection of Autumn/Winter 1995 was a controversial comment on what he termed the 'rape' of Scotland by the British, a theme he was to revisit with the 'Widows of Culloden' collection of Autumn/Winter 2006. The later period of the Victorian Raj inspired his collection 'The Girl Who Lived in the Tree' of Autumn/Winter 2008. McQueen built fanciful themes and narratives by melding different historical and cultural reference points to create the new, the beautiful and, often, the dark.

Opposite A flapper-inspired dress by
John Galliano, Spring/Summer 2008.

Above Women in the 1920s wearing
the fashionable flapper dresses
of the period.

Right An original 1920s flapper dress.

Opposite **Romantic, historically inspired gown by Vivienne Westwood, Autumn/Winter 2006.**

Right *Lady in Red* **by Nicolaes Maes (1634–93).**

Below **Original Victorian gown,** *c.* **1890.**

Vivienne Westwood often draws inspiration from eighteenth-century portraiture by the likes of Fragonard, with its mood of romance and eroticism; she also turns to Classical drapery, Highland dress and a large number of other immediately recognizable components from historical clothing and art through the centuries, both real and fanciful, many of which she has made her own signature references. Her rather idealistic and romantic view may be summed up in her quote, '…it's so important to look to the past. Because people did have taste, and they had ideals of excellence, and those things are not going to come back unless people look at the past.' On her 'Anglomania' ranges from 1993 to 1994, her press department reveals that Westwood believes that fashion is a combination and exchange of ideas between France and England: 'On the English side we have tailoring and an easy charm, on the French side that solidity of design and proportion that comes from never being satisfied because something can always be done to make it better, more refined.'

VINTAGE RETRO Vintage and retro clothing can be a great source of inspiration for the designer: real clothes with real details, trims and construction methods are invaluable as research in a great many ways. They can inform the silhouette, construction, colour, pattern and trim of a new garment and evoke a period in history. Indeed, sometimes history can be pretty much defined by fashion: a hemline, a shoulder or a particular pattern on a specific fabric can all speak to the informed of an item's date and place of manufacture. Designers, of any discipline, should make themselves fully aware of what has gone before in order to move design forward.

Vintage clothing shops, antique and specialist clothing fairs, charity shops or an elderly relative's wardrobe are all great sources for vintage clothing. Eras can be defined by fashion details alone – the low waists and straight-cut silhouettes of 1920s flapper dresses, the bias cut of the 1930s and the wartime economy of the 1940s, followed by the full-skirted look of the 1950s. The 1960s saw a return to the straight silhouette of the 1920s but with a dash of space race thrown in and with synthetic fabrics becoming widely used for the first time. The 1970s saw a hippy influence with longer, more flowing skirts and dresses in natural colours and a re-emergence of the colour orange, not much seen in fashion since the 1920s. The 1980s have become best known for the power-dressing look, with sharp shoulders and short, tight skirts: a look that truly meant business. Fashion continues to reinvent by looking back but without copying slavishly what has gone before; new elements are brought into play but there remains an inescapable feel of the times in which the originals were created. According to Andrew Groves, course director at the University of Westminster, London, 'Primary research into actual garments is vitally important if research isn't just going to be about style and surface. Many designers design from 2D imagery – from either a

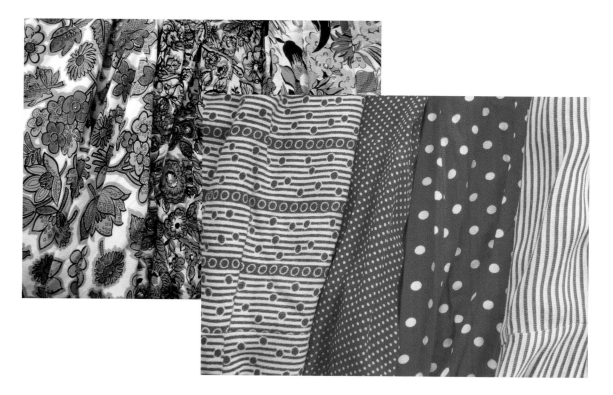

magazine or a book – but others understand that garments are 3D and that therefore to learn from and to design from, a flat 2D image cannot give the level and depth that an actual garment can. As fantastic as a Cecil Beaton image of a Dior evening gown is, actually studying the inside of such a garment can be so much more inspiring and rewarding. Through the study and reference of previous methods of cut and construction a reinterpretation of that language can be developed and quoted from. This doesn't need to be restricted to haute couture vintage dresses; in fact any clothing from a previous era can be a highly rewarding source of inspiration; be it designer end, mass market, utilitarian or uniform. All have unique ways in which the period of their make and design will have affected the choice of fabric, finish and cut. Indeed, the garment found in a vintage shop or charity store can often be far more rewarding and have a far more interesting take on whatever the actual fashion was at the time of its design. In a time when 2D imagery of the last hundred years has been used, appropriated, referenced and represented a thousand times and then spread throughout the Internet, it's the uniqueness of these garments that can bring a fresh approach to a designer's research process.'

Opposite top **The interior of Lotty, a Tokyo retro shop.**

Opposite bottom **A selection of clothes in Beyond Retro, a vintage clothing store in London.**

Above **1930s and 1940s vintage textiles showing a variety of period patterns and prints.**

THE LANGUAGE OF CLOTHES

Every type of garment and clothing has its own vocabulary, specifics of construction, cut and finish that define it in the bigger picture of fashion design and clothing.

Rules can be broken, of course, but a knowledge of this language of clothes is essential to good design; once a designer is fully versed in this formal system, this vocabulary, they can go on to subvert it, to play with it, to further add to their creative output. It is akin to the abstract artist's having honed his or her skills in traditional painting and drawing techniques in order then to convincingly abstract line, form and colour.

What is it that defines tailoring, or sportswear, or workwear; what methods of construction and finish are peculiar to denim, to shirting or to military uniform? It is via thorough observation and careful study that this knowledge is gained and it forms a vital part of fashion education.

On construction and construction techniques, illustrator and lecturer Richard Gray identifies the development and analysis of traditional techniques as being vital for research: 'There is an over-reliance on technology and machinery to produce work that is traditionally done by hand. The two should work together, in terms of both understanding the integrity of the source, and discovering what inspiring new things can be achieved with it through technology and modernization.'

Take the length of stitch and the way the seams are treated: are they pressed open, one way, how many rows, what is their width, are they topstitched and/or stitched through, are they a matching or contrast colour, how thick is the thread? This may all sound mundane, or even obsessive, but such elements are the very vocabulary of the language of clothes. They all add up to what makes specific clothing types recognizable and unique.

Certain companies and designers have added their own signatures to this language; details and manufacturing techniques, often uniquely their own, have evolved – the triple rows of topstitching on rugged Carhartt utility pieces, the signature hand-stitched-through label at Margiela, the jacket hanger-on-outside at Gaultier, the signature stitching on the back pocket of a pair of Levi's jeans. A Comme des Garçons shirt is recognizable by its tiny felled side seams, the width of the topstitching on the collar and the shape of the top pocket. While other design elements evolve and change constantly within their shirting range, these things remain a constant: the core language of their shirt brand.

Willie Walters, course director of the fashion BA at Central Saint Martins, says on this subject: 'Our second project in the first year is a shirt project, whereby students really start to think about collars, set-in sleeves, buttonholes. The idea of that is that you don't know what you don't know … we do say to the students that arrive with technical and construction skills, say from China, Japan or Germany, you can put the collar wherever you like, it can go round the hem if you like; whereas if you've never made a shirt before it's more sensible to put the collar around the neck, to learn those necessary skills, to take your designing further.'

Above **A woman wearing breeches at Tattersall's horse auction in London, 1938.**

Above right **An image from a 1940s American magazine featuring ladies' breeches.**

Right **Original 1940s ladies' breeches.**

Above **Smocking mood board by Sam Towner, University of Westminster, London.**

Right and below (detail) **Original 19th-century smock, Benenden Collection, Kingston University, London.**

Opposite **Children wearing traditional smocks in the 19th century. Photograph by John Cimon Warburg.**

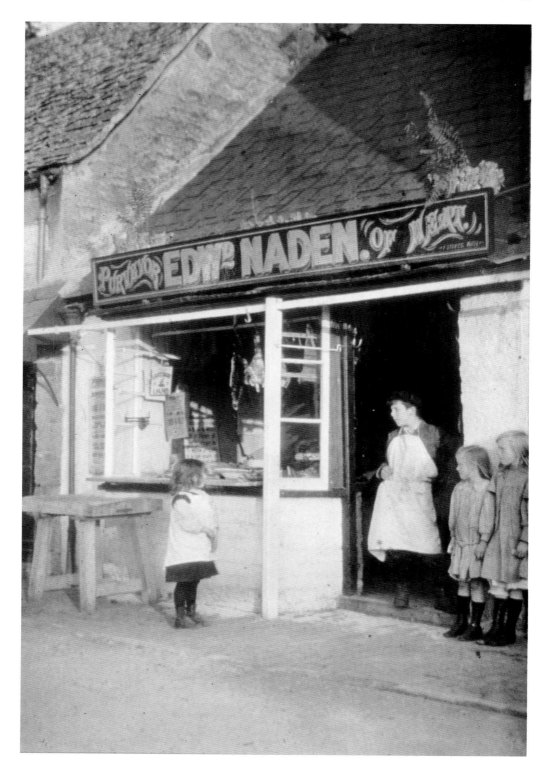

54

Garments from the Benenden
Collection at Kingston University,
London, a rich research resource
for students.

ARCHIVE   Many designers, educational establishments and companies put together an archive. This might include garments from past production, 'source' garments (such as interesting historical or traditional garments that have been bought in), and vintage and retro pieces that are considered inspirational. From these the designers might draw ideas for details, such as a pocket design, embroidery style, collar shape or overall silhouette. The sort of knowledge gained from careful study is vital to a greater understanding of the discipline of fashion and clothing design. Talking about the Benenden Collection of vintage clothing housed at Kingston University, Elinor Renfrew, head of Kingston's fashion course, says: 'Historical research is underused, not referenced enough. It is the core of their business, which is why I consider the Benenden archive so important for Kingston University; it references what has gone before, what is good about what has gone before: this is how reinvention happens. It is this knowledge that really separates the good designers from the not so good, and is at the very heart of the academic basis of fashion education. A designer without a good knowledge of fashion history is only half formed.'

Sportswear Company (SPW) is an Italian firm that owns Stone Island and previously owned C.P. Company. At its headquarters located in Ravarino, near Modena, Italy, the company has huge warehouses full of not only its own archive of garments going back thirty-five years but also of other utilitarian garments, which they use for research. Both Stone Island and C.P.

Company were founded by the designer Massimo Osti, who wanted to design menswear that was functional and practical, using the most innovative fabrics and manufacturing techniques. The archives that he built up can be used to reference ideas, styles and details from previous collections and also to revisit ideas as new technologies are created. For companies such as this the design process is about developing from previous products, not constantly reinventing from scratch each season. So inspirational is this archive and process that it has given rise to a new menswear label known as MA.STRUM, designed by Donrad Duncan in collaboration with the Massimo Osti Studio. Duncan has created experimental yet functional pieces of technical outerwear inspired by the technical genius of the fabrics and treatments stored in Osti's textile archive.

MUSEUMS The world's museums and galleries remain one of the most valuable resources for the designer and researcher. According to illustrator and lecturer Richard Gray, a major source of inspiration for the designer is 'any museum, or any place which gives you access to the authentic source of information, not just printed visual depictions of it: the Victoria and Albert Museum, the Wellcome Collection, flea markets and vintage shops.' Designer Paul Smith says: 'As such anything can inspire, but in terms of actual research most museums will allow you to look at their archives or give you specific information provided you plan it well in advance and make an appointment. People don't realize the opportunity there is to talk to curators or researchers and to delve into the archives.' He urges researchers not to forget, 'not strictly speaking museums, but the Royal Institute of British Architects, for instance, has an amazing photographic archive, as I'm sure places like the British Film Institute also do.'

On museums and the changing face of visual research in fashion and fashion education, designer and lecturer Andrew Ibi advises, 'There is much to be learned from what's happening around us, we know from the past that today is the research topic for tomorrow. So it's really about looking around and taking it in. The Internet is a fantastic tool, though very few individuals are able to harness its energy in a challenging and effective way, it's always too passive, but as a result museums and libraries are out of fashion and are underused. Private collections are often inaccessible but ... often first-hand recollections and accounts can be heard from the collector. It's about finding unearthed topics that have been forgotten about or overlooked.'

Opposite top **Sleeve detail,** *c.* 1830.

Opposite bottom and right **Two 18th-century panniered dresses, displayed in the Fashion and Textiles Museum in Bath, England.**

Below **Richly decorated historical clothing displayed in the Los Angeles County Museum of Art, California: a lady's mantle, 1891 (left), and a coat and waistcoat, 1760 (right).**

Historically, many museum collections grow out of personal collections that have been bequeathed. Many museums and galleries now have online resources, with their collections catalogued and photographed, making it quick and easy to find a particular style of dress or period; and in some cases they might feature pieces from their archives that are not available to view at the museum itself. In addition to the permanent exhibits, most galleries put on shows on specific and specialized themes; these might be of particular designers, periods in history or types of clothing or textiles, and talks and workshops are often run in conjunction with any particular exhibition.

Below A fashion gallery in the Philadelphia Museum of Art.

Above The exterior of the Philadelphia Museum of Art during its Schiaparelli exhibition in 2003.

Above A fashion gallery at the Fashion and Textiles Museum in Bath, England.

Top At the Washington Textiles Museum, a display of Central Asian ikats in the Colours of the Oasis gallery.

ART AS INSPIRATION

Since the early twentieth century, fashion designers have often looked to fine art for inspiration. In the 1920s Paris couturier Paul Poiret responded to Léon Bakst's fabulous costume designs for the Ballets Russes, while Elsa Schiaparelli is well known for her collaborations with the Surrealist artists Salvador Dalí and Jean Cocteau. Indeed, the very silhouette of 1920s fashion was Cubist in nature, tubular and streamlined, much in the spirit of the stylized paintings of Tamara de Lempicka.

During the late 1930s and early 1940s, creativity was stifled in Europe because of the war, but in the United States, Gilbert Adrian was to create pieces based on Picasso-esque motifs and shapes. In the postwar period, the new art movements were to have a great influence on fashion in Paris and London and around the world. In the 1960s French designers André Courrèges and Paco Rabanne were heavily influenced by the monochrome palette of Op art and by space-related themes, while London's Mary Quant made the Pop art daisy motif her own. In London the Mr Freedom boutiques showcased bright, fun clothes inspired by the new Pop art in both the US and the UK; clothes of comic-strip prints and bright colours recalled the work of Andy Warhol, while such companies as Biba were at the forefront of the Art Deco revival.

Art-inspired headwear by Stephen Jones at an exhibition of his work at MOMU, Antwerp, Belgium, in 2010–11.

Yves Saint Laurent was acutely aware of the boutique explosion, and capitalized with the introduction of prêt-à-porter (ready-to-wear), using many of the Pop motifs in his own work; the cutouts of Henri Matisse and the grid paintings of Piet Mondrian also featured in his creative output of the 1960s and 1970s.

Alexander McQueen was much influenced by modern art, especially the photography of Joel-Peter Witkin and Hans Bellmer, the sculpture of Rebecca Horn and Anish Kapoor and the mixed-media artworks of Damien Hirst. Conversely, a designer such as Vivienne Westwood is much more likely to be inspired by the art of the past – the romantic portraits and idealized landscapes of Fragonard or Gainsborough. John Galliano has looked back to the Surrealist works of Man Ray and Jean Cocteau. Rei Kawakubo of Comme des Garçons regularly collaborates with contemporary artists, using their imagery in the company's advertising and for her website; recent collaborators include Mondongo, the Quay Brothers and the Chinese artist Ai Weiwei.

Sharon Graubard of Stylesight writes: 'Nobody uses colour like a fine artist. If you want to see new combinations for colour-blocking or stripes, look at

Kenneth Noland and Josef Albers. If you want to use sparkle and shine, look at Damien Hirst, Anish Kapoor. Look at artists for T-shirt graphics, for finishing techniques, for typography, for surface texture'.

As the whole business of research for design has evolved, mainly through fashion education, it is interesting to note that designers no longer necessarily dwell on one, recognizable theme. They might pick an obscure art movement and mix it with other, disparate elements to create a narrative; or be inspired, perhaps, by just one painting, and even then not necessarily one well known to the public. It has become much more about the design process than presenting the public with reworkings of already familiar elements. On this theme, Stephanie Cooper, lecturer at Central Saint Martins, considers art to be an absolutely key area of research for the student, and cites as fonts of inspiration: 'Artists who consider the human body, both present and absent in their work, such as Marc Quinn, Antony Gormley and Christian Boltanski. Anatomical studies and sculpture utilizing casting of body parts. Sculptors and painters that challenge preconceptions regarding gender and beauty such as Louise Bourgeois, Hans Bellmer and Jenny Saville. Artists working with investigating dynamic spatial awareness, art movements that define the spirit of the times and photographers who capture the human condition in all its guises – August Sander, Diane Arbus and Cindy Sherman.'

Yves Saint Laurent 1960s Mondrian-inspired dress shown here in the 2004 retrospective show in New York.

SURREALISM Surrealism continues to be fashion's best-loved art movement. Initially based on concepts, it soon became preoccupied with the portrayal of beauty, distortion and the human body – the perfect vehicle for fashion.

As early as 1919 Max Ernst became acutely aware of the newly emerging creative force that was fashion design, and appropriated the imagery of the mannequin and dressmaker for his work. This was the machine age, and the sewing machine became a potent motif in Surrealist art, appearing in the works of Salvador Dalí, Joseph Cornell and Man Ray, among others. Thus the links with fashion were forged, and the two disciplines became bedfellows.

In Paris, the Italian fashion designer Elsa Schiaparelli embarked on her fashion career with knitted trompe l'oeil sweaters, with definite Surrealist undertones, and went on to forge friendships and working relationships with many of the artists of the day. Schiaparelli had studied painting and sculpture, and her new fashion aesthetic was moulded by the Surrealists including Dalí, Jean Cocteau and René Magritte. Her two collaborations with Dalí in 1937 have become iconic fashion pieces: the Lobster Dress, with its provocative printed lobster; and the Tears Dress, with printed trompe l'oeil rips, pre-empting by several decades the punk ethic of the 1970s and the subsequent slashing and deconstruction of the 1980s and 1990s. Each bore a direct relationship to a work by Dalí, with the Lobster Dress referencing the *Lobster Telephone* of 1936, and the Tears Dress seen in similar form in the 1936 painting *Three Young Surrealist Women Holding in their Arms the Skins of an Orchestra*. Schiaparelli attracted many famous customers, and the Lobster Dress was photographed by Cecil Beaton for *Vogue* in the spring of 1937, as worn by the Duchess of Windsor, formerly Wallis Simpson. There were also notable collaborations with Cocteau: an evening coat embroidered with profiles forming the shape of a vase with roses atop, and a cross-over evening jacket, from autumn 1937, featuring a profile head of a woman with her embroidered hair falling down one sleeve. Fashion owes Schiaparelli and the Surrealists a great debt: their combined imagery is enduring, and is still regularly employed by today's designers, art directors and advertisers.

A group of images showing a single Surrealist motif, that of a lobster, as employed by an artist and designers: Salvador Dalí's *Lobster Telephone*, 1936 (opposite), Schiaparelli's Lobster Dress, 1937 (left) and a lobster hat by French designer Eric Halley (though usually attributed to Philip Treacy), worn by Isabella Blow, *c.* 1998 (above).

Above Original 1970s vintage trompe l'oeil T-shirt.

Left Trompe l'oeil jacket from the Comme des Garçons Autumn/Winter 2009 collection.

Opposite 1920s trompe l'oeil bow sweater by Schiaparelli.

TROMPE L'OEIL

Trompe l'oeil, as an artistic technique, dates back to the times of ancient Greece and Rome, and was used in wall murals to trick the eye into believing the unreal – an open door leading elsewhere, a window with a view, the heavens opening on a ceiling. With advances in the discovery of perspective during the Renaissance, the technique became more elaborate, and trompe l'oeil (French for 'deceive the eye') flourished as an art form.

It first appeared in fashion in the 1920s with Schiaparelli's hand-knitted black jumpers with white bows. She described her now famous sweater in her 1954 autobiography, *Shocking Life*: 'So I drew a large butterfly bow in front, like a scarf around the neck – the primitive drawing of a child in prehistoric times', explaining that 'the bow must be white against a black ground'. Another of her trompe l'oeil inventions was the printing of newsprint on to fabric, which was to be later adopted as a signature technique by designer John Galliano.

Many of today's designers return again and again to trompe l'oeil, clearly in love with the wit and irony of the deception. At Chanel, Karl Lagerfeld employs the technique to turn flat fabrics into tweeds and to embellish garments with what appear to be lavish amounts of jewelry, but which in fact is embroidery. Gaultier adds jackets to bodices, and Marc Jacobs embroiders trompe l'oeil underwear to chiffon dresses. Sonia Rykiel meanwhile pushes the sweater idea on further to create dresses with faux belts, bows and buttons, very much in the style of that Schiaparelli sweater that clearly still inspires her some eighty years later.

The Belgian designer Martin Margiela uses the technique in a much more esoteric manner, typical of his style; a 'Chesterfield' jacket, inspired by a sofa, has printed deep buttoning and tufting, while simple jersey dresses are printed as beaded 1920s flapper dresses, or to appear as chunky knits. He uses the technique regularly on T-shirts, with numerous different items printed to the neckline in the trompe l'oeil manner – all in a rather more sophisticated style, perhaps, than the ubiquitous tuxedo T-shirt of the 1970s.

OP ART Op art, the art of optical and visual illusion, numbered Bridget Riley and
Victor Vasarely among its chief exponents, and was quickly picked up on
by the fashion and textile designers of the 1960s. The strong, frequently
black-and-white, graphic element suited the futuristic mood of the times.
Large and bold graphics sat well with the geometric simple shapes of the
shift dresses of the 1960s. Such designers as Paco Rabanne and Courrèges
in Paris, and Mary Quant in London favoured the monochrome palette, a
perennial fashion favourite for a high-impact and dramatic look.

Current designers who have looked at Op art for inspiration in the last few years include Raf Simons at Jil Sander, Anna Sui, Matthew Williamson and Gareth Pugh.

Somewhere between Op art and trompe l'oeil lies the work of M. C. Escher, a Dutch graphic artist who worked in the mid-twentieth century. His hands eerily drawing each other and his impossible-to-build classical-style buildings with never-ending staircases have become iconic. Alexander McQueen was inspired by Escher for prints where dogtooth checks morphed Escher-style into birds in the New Look-inspired collection of Autumn/Winter 2009.

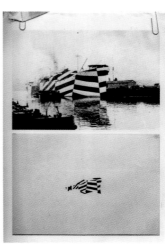

Opposite top *Bora III*, by Victor Vasarely.

Opposite bottom Op art-inspired research in sketchbooks by Aaron Tubb, University of Westminster, London.

Right An Op art-inspired offering from Gareth Pugh's Spring/Summer 2011 collection.

Below Op art-inspired original vintage garments.

UNIFORMS

The upper classes were the first to identify themselves on the battlefield, by means of heraldry. As armour disappeared, identification of friend and foe became problematic. It broke down badly in the English Civil War of the seventeenth century, when Parliament and King fielded armies that were initially almost indistinguishable; when uniforms were introduced, they were regiment-wide, each colonel being responsible for clothing and equipping his men. Coats had wide turned-back cuffs that provided a second colour, so that regiments could be distinguished by colour. Oliver Cromwell's New Model Army wore the first army-wide uniform, its foot soldiers dressed in red coats. When the British Army was formed after the disbanding of the New Model Army, it would be forever after uniformly dressed.

Since then uniform has not just been functional. It carries identificatory and display elements as well, all contributing to making it one of the richest and largest areas of clothing design research for the designer. Whether it be the pomp of a Napoleonic uniform, with its scarlet jacket, plumes and gold braid, the functionality of the flying suit with its numerous pockets and rows of stitching, or the colours of a medal bar, all can feed the designer's imagination and inform their designs.

Below **Marc Jacobs for Louis Vuitton Spring/Summer 2010 collection, with uniform-inspired pieces.**

Opposite top **Uniform-inspired mood board by Emma Lines, University of Westminster, London.**

Opposite bottom left **Some of the large variety of images to be found on formation flashes (badges) during the Second World War are shown on this army scarf, stitched on by one soldier after being demobbed and kept as a souvenir. The number and variety made the scarf a highly sought-after collector's item.**

Opposite bottom right **Interior shot of WCAGA retro store, New York, showing some of the vintage uniform stocked.**

Clockwise from above **Junya Watanabe**
uniform-inspired coat from his
Autumn/Winter 2010 collection;
World War One soldier in uniform; an
American serviceman tucking into a
pan of baked beans, Italy, May 1944;
Second World War field jacket.

Opposite Mood board by Rachel Raheja,
University of Westminster, London.

COMBAT UNIFORM   The tradition for brightly coloured, instantly recognizable battlefield dress changed first with the green and grey uniforms worn by the British Army riflemen of the eighteenth century. By 1845 khaki had been adopted by British troops in India, the word deriving from the Hindustani and Urdu words for 'dusty', and by 1902, in both the United States and Britain, the red jacket had been totally abandoned for all but ceremonial wear. Russia followed in 1908, in 1909 Italy employed grigio-verde ('grey-green') and the following year Germany adopted feldgrau ('field grey') for its uniforms.

At the onset of the First World War a few countries still went to battle in uniforms of national colours – the French, for example, wore blue jackets and red trousers, but this was soon abandoned to be replaced by 'horizon blue'. Other nations followed with various shades of grey, blue and drab green.

From the muddy trenches of the Somme to the dusty deserts of the Middle East, the terrain in dispute has now come to determine the colour of uniform worn in a given situation, from the point of view of either concealment or recognition.

'What late twentieth-century soldiers saw as soldierly tasks ranged from the intuitively obvious, such things as weapon handling, fieldcraft, and the effective driving of military vehicles both on and off roads, to other, less practical, aspects that were nonetheless important ingredients of being "soldierly". A highly valued element … was looking the part. For a soldier to be convincing, to cut the right figure, his military clothing and equipment had to fit properly and he had to wear it in a soldierly way. This went beyond the simply utilitarian. At various times I have seen … "creases" sewn down the front and back of combat trousers to make them appear pressed, or light cotton jungle sweat rags used as neck cloths in chilly European winters to show that the wearer had jungle experience. Over and over again I have seen soldiers buy equipment and gadgets because they … considered them better than what were issued, whether they were or not. Some soldierly attributes and skills were less obvious – for example, lighting a cigarette or a cooking fire in high winds and heavy rain, keeping one's kit dry in the field, cooking military rations with a palatable result, holding one's liquor on a night out, and attracting women. All these aspects comprised a rich mixture, combining craft, art, skill, experience, knowledge, and ideas of masculinity, all used as defining elements in being a "soldier".'

Red Coat, Green Machine: Continuity in Change in the British Army 1700 to 2000, Charles Kirke, 2009

Below Mood board by Rora Chow,
University of Westminster, London.

Right The traditional red and gold
livery of the Yeomen of the Guard, a
ceremonial bodyguard to the Queen.

Below right Original vintage uniforms,
probably those of bandsmen.

CEREMONIAL UNIFORM There remains a dazzling array of ceremonial uniforms throughout the
world, frozen pieces of history steeped in tradition and ceremony. They
might be those of the police, marines, Yeomen Warders, sailors, heralds
or bandsmen, each with their own unique decoration and colours, imbued
with significance to the wearer. One man's outrageous headgear might
be another's hallowed tradition.

Top Herald's uniform (Officer of Arms) at Hand & Lock (see pages 32–33).

Above Vintage uniform.

Left In his Spring/Summer collection of 2009, John Galliano, as his first outfit, sent out this red suit, complete with a Stephen Jones hat inspired by the bearskin cap of the Guards.

Left Mood board by Amanda Svart, University of Westminster, London.

Below left Tropical uniform-inspired shirt dress by Phoebe Philo for Céline, Spring/Summer 2010.

Below Original Yves Saint Laurent Rive Gauche safari jacket from the 1960s, stored in the Benenden Collection at Kingston University, London.

Bottom Vintage tropical US Army shirt.

TROPICAL UNIFORM

Tropical uniform, like most uniform, was born out of necessity – dressing for warfare in tropical or desert regions. For the latter, it was sand-coloured and functional, with capacious pockets, belts and often shorts in place of trousers, and originally included the pith helmet to protect against the sun.

Yves Saint Laurent, ever sensitive to the zeitgeist, had created the first formal trouser suits for women in 1966, giving a sense of empowerment to women at a time when the feminist movement was starting to grow in strength; it was a period of female emancipation not seen – in fashion terms – since corsets were abandoned in the early part of the twentieth century. In 1967, in his 'African' collection, Saint Laurent added to these suits with military detailing inspired by tropical uniform, including bellowed pockets, eyelets and topstitching. He utilized the muted palette of desert and jungle fatigues – beiges, tans and khakis – and accessorized with Sam Browne belts, D-rings and straw hats. This was one of the first times a fashion designer had looked outside mainstream fashion for details and references to bring to their work to this extent, and was quite revolutionary. The safari suit as a fashion item was born, and was to be much copied for many years to come.

In the years since Saint Laurent first brought tropical uniform-inspired fashion to the catwalk any overtly military connotations have begun to play second fiddle to a feeling of a relaxed tropical elegance. This look has been updated and successfully employed by designers such as Phoebe Philo at Céline, as seen in her elegant, easy coat dress with epaulettes, bellowed pockets and tabs for the Spring/Summer 2010 collection shown here.

Above **Desert warfare: American and British forces preparing for war against Iraq.**

CAMOUFLAGE 'Camouflage' derives from the French word *camouflet*, referring to smoke blown in someone's eyes to blind or confuse them. The first military application of camouflage – or disruptive pattern material (DPM), as it is technically known – in a painted or printed form was in the early twentieth century. Lucien-Victor Guirand de Scévola, a Parisian portrait artist serving with the artillery at north-eastern France in 1914, was the first artist to disguise big guns, followed by many other French artists including Marcel Bain, Jean-Louis Forain and Abel Truchet. Under de Scévola, a specialist camouflage section was set up that employed artists and hundreds of civilians, known as *camofleurs*.

A year later Britain followed their lead, and by 1916 had started a

camouflage section with Solomon J. Solomon, a prolific artist and illustrator of the day, as key adviser. The first British Army camouflage overalls went into production in 1918: a sniper suit and a boiler suit.

Unsurprisingly, since artists were very much at the heart of its development, the design of camouflage shifted from an Impressionistic style to a style much more influenced by Cubism – even this functional military technique being subject to the vagaries of design and fashion.

The term 'Dazzle' had been used for certain types of camouflage during the First World War, used on ships and designed to mislead rather than to conceal. The term reappeared on the social scene in Britain in the immediate postwar years. In London, the Chelsea Arts Club held a Dazzle Ball, while at the Royal Albert Hall in March 1919 partygoers in camouflage costumes danced beneath balloons painted to look like bombs: this was the first documented appearance of camouflage as fashionable dress.

With the onset of the Second World War in 1939, the British Surrealist artist Roland Penrose wrote *The Home Guard Manual of Camouflage*, and was involved with the army's Camouflage Development and Training Centre: again the contemporary art scene played a part in camouflage development.

By 1961 camouflage was being replaced by plain-coloured suits, not only as the West turned its back on the combat gear of the war years, but because of problems of manufacture – it became increasingly difficult even to get the cloth printed. However, camouflage was to reappear later in the 1960s, and by 1972 had become universal army issue.

The American 'chocolate chip' desert camouflage was developed in the early 1970s and was to become associated with the Gulf War of 1991, to be discontinued shortly afterwards. It would re-emerge as issue for the Iraqi army following the American invasion of 2003.

Away from the arena of war itself, camouflage was adopted by anti-war protesters of the 1970s, including the Vietnam War veterans. It fast became a potent symbol of war employed for anti-war protest.

In 1986 in New York Andy Warhol made a series of prints re-colouring the USM81 camouflage in bright, Pop art colours, and these were used the following year by designer Stephen Sprouse for his fashion collection.

Around the same time camouflage was also being appropriated in street

fashion – trends inspired not by the catwalk but by the streets. As well as being functional and utilitarian, camouflage clothing had an aggressive edge. Popular types of camouflage in street fashion were British DPM; American desert chocolate chip and woodland, and Swiss red Leibermuster.

In a huge reversal of how the fashion scene more usually works, designers were now looking to the street for inspiration, and camouflage found its way on to the catwalk. Versace, Paul Smith, Yohji Yamamoto, Jean Paul Gaultier, Junya Watanabe, Christopher Kane, Prada, McQueen and Louis Vuitton have all used or reinvented disruptive pattern material for their individual house styles.

Opposite top **Two soldiers of the French Marine Infantry Parachute Regiment camouflaging each other in preparation for a training exercise.**

Opposite bottom **Camouflage fabric swatches in a student sketchbook, by Aaron Tubb, University of Westminster, London.**

Left **Camouflage fabric coat by Junya Watanabe, Autumn/Winter 2010.**

THE TRENCH COAT

The exact origins of the trench coat are contested, with both Burberry and Aquascutum claiming its invention as their own. Developed as a lighter alternative to the heavy greatcoat worn by troops in the First World War, the first recorded design was submitted to the British War Office in 1901 by Burberry. It was an optional piece of kit for the British Army and only worn by the senior ranks. The coat had D-rings and straps for the attachment of epaulettes, lanyards and other insignia, and the rings on the belt were for the attachment of map holders and swords.

The name 'trench coat' was coined by the front-line troops, and many of them bought their coats home after the war, when they began to be worn in a civilian context and became very much a fashion staple. Both Aquascutum and Burberry produced the waterproof garments for men and women, and in the United States as early as 1918 *Harper's Bazaar* was advertising them 'for women in service at home and abroad'.

The armies of most countries produced their own versions of the wet-weather coat, and it was still being worn by officers at the time of the Second World War, although developments in warfare necessitated the change to shorter jackets, such as the British Denison and the US Army's field jackets, which allowed for much more freedom of movement.

By this point, the trench coat was typically double-breasted with raglan sleeves, epaulettes and a belt with D-rings, and usually seen in khaki, beige or black – a formula that has changed little.

Its origins lend the coat a certain air of authority and it has been much employed in film and fiction, comic-book hero Dick Tracy and Bogart's character in *Casablanca* both lending it an unmistakable cool.

With the renaissance of heritage brands Burberry and Aquascutum in the 1990s, the trench coat was again very much at the forefront of fashion, a true classic that has been subject to endless reworking and reinvention.

Above **Original vintage trench coats on a market stall.**

Right **1918 advertisement from** *Harper's Bazaar* **featuring an early ladies' trench coat.**

Opposite **Updated classic trench coat from the Burberry Autumn/Winter 2009, designed by Christopher Bailey.**

HARPER'S BAZAR
November, 1918
page 88
GIFTS FOR *the* WOMAN *in* SERVICE *at* HOME *and* ABROAD

The top-coat, frequently the most convincing badge of service, is smart when made of tan cravenetted serge, interlined with flannel and lined with serge. $65. Seperate fleece lining to button in, $25. extra.

HERITAGE

Many modern fashion brands are built on heritage, be it real or perceived. Different brands invoke different heritage spirits. They might be national, historical, lifestyle or sporting, evoking a certain era and often a certain place, feeding nostalgia and speaking of quality and finer times. The pool of imagery is bountiful and rich, and can be subtly altered to suit shifting trends. It can move around a country and across a century, yet still somehow remain true to a particular brand ethic. This might be one of youth, luxury, health or quality. Consider Ralph Lauren's polo and tennis players, Abercrombie's healthy and active teenagers or Burberry's bright young things. These are all inventions, but are immediately recognizable. Nostalgia is a powerful force: once described as a medical condition, it is certainly no longer that, but it is a great selling tool. The imagery used in advertising will often be the same as that used for design research, all reinforcing the look of the season or collection.

A company such as Abercrombie & Fitch will give each season's collection a fresh name, placing it, perhaps, in a different time and place (in the case of Abercrombie, always in North America), the clothes remaining true to the look of the brand. This spirit and images associated with it make up the starting point for research, and might trigger ideas for colour, fabric, graphics and texture; and any clothing in the imagery might also do the same. This imagery could be from photography, archive, film, advertising, or the brand's own history.

Many of the luxury brands look back over their own history for inspiration. For example, Louis Vuitton was founded in 1854, and clearly has a rich past to draw from. Others, such as Aquascutum, have used

their history very successfully to relaunch or reinforce their profile in today's marketplace.

A sense of a designer's national identity might also be invoked by the use of certain imagery, a flag, a textile, something quintessentially of a given nation's heritage: Vivienne Westwood's tartan, Ralph Lauren's invocation of the Star-Spangled Banner, or Gaultier's French matelot stripes.

Burberry was founded in 1856 when twenty-one-year-old Thomas Burberry, a former draper's apprentice, opened his own store in the English town of Basingstoke in Hampshire. By 1870, the business had established itself by focusing on the development of outdoor wear. In 1880, Burberry introduced clothing made of gabardine, a hardwearing, water-resistant yet breathable fabric, in which the yarn is waterproofed before weaving. In 1891, Burberry opened a shop in the Haymarket, London, which still exists.

The now-iconic logo of a knight on horseback together with the word prorsum, Latin for 'forwards', was first registered as a trademark in 1901; Prorsum is now used as the name for the ready-to-wear line. The Burberry brand became synonymous with outerwear, and indeed the outerwear pieces remain the defining part of any modern Burberry presentation. Burberry was the outfitter for Roald Amundsen's South Pole expedition in 1911, as well as Ernest Shackleton's 1914 Antarctic expedition. British mountaineer George Mallory wore a Burberry gabardine jacket on his ill-fated attempt on Everest in 1924.

Burberry's chief executive, Christopher Bailey, was asked, in an interview with journalist Sally Bain in the magazine *westminsterfashion* in 2009, 'What are the constants within Burberry, regardless of seasonal variations?' He replied: 'Outerwear and all our different iconic coats from duffels, to pea coats, to fisherman cabans to trench coats. Britishness, because to me Burberry is about as British as they come. Heritage: 152 years of history that you just don't find anywhere else.'

THE STARS AND STRIPES: FRANCE, FRIDAY, MARCH 15, 1918

BURBERRYS
Military Outfitters
8 Boulevard Malesherbes, PARIS

SUPPLY
AMERICAN OFFICERS
Direct—or through their AGENTS
behind the lines with every necessary
Article of War Equipment.

TRENCH WARMS
TUNICS & BREECHES
OVERCOATS
IMPERMEABLES
TRENCH CAPS
SAM BROWNE BELTS
INSIGNIA etc., etc.

BEST QUALITY at
REASONABLE PRICES.

AGENTS IN FRANCE
Holding Stocks of Burberry Goods.

Opposite **Louis Vuitton store window featuring their trademark luxury luggage.**

Above **Early vintage Barbour advertisement.**

Right **Early Burberry trench coat advertisement.**

82

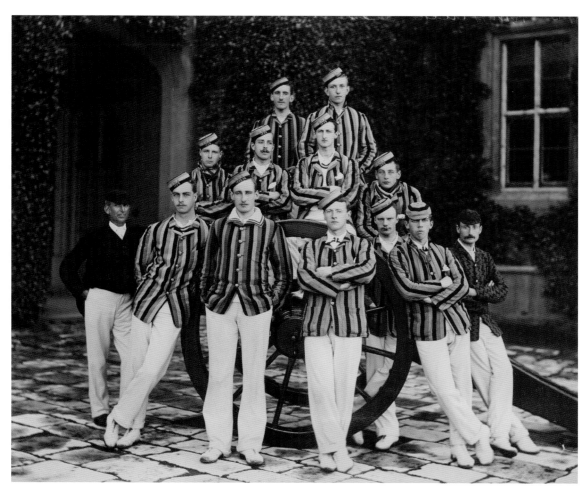

Top **Royal Military Academy cricketers,
1894**, wearing wonderful striped and
patterned blazers.

Above left and right **Vintage school
striped scarves and multicoloured
caps.**

Within what we might call heritage, and the associated brands, there is any number of places one could look for inspiration for design. Here, the stripes of the college scarf and schoolboy blazer are shown as an example.

School uniform and university colours provide good reference for colour and stripes for both the fashion and the textile designer. The often idiosyncratic mix of colours in club blazers, boater bands and college scarves provides great inspiration as well as being evocative of bygone eras of long summer days in the city of dreaming spires, boating regattas and punting on the River Cam.

Striped school-uniform-inspired blazer from Balenciaga, Autumn/Winter 2007.

SAVILE ROW   Savile Row, lying to the north of Regent Street in London's West End, is the historical and spiritual home of gentlemen's tailoring; tailors have operated from this street since the 1730s, and the term 'bespoke' is said to have originated there.

In its long history it has claimed kings, movie stars and maharajahs among its customer base, and its reputation as the world destination for handmade tailoring, sometimes thought to be shaky, seems now once again to be secure.

Hollywood was always attracted to Savile Row. In the 1920s screen idol Rudolph Valentino was dressed by Anderson and Sheppard, as were Marlene Dietrich and the dapper Noël Coward. Later, movie mogul Louis B. Meyer selected Kilgour, French and Stanbury as his tailors of choice, along with the likes of Edward G. Robinson, Rex Harrison, David Niven and Frank Sinatra. In 1959 Kilgour created Cary Grant's suits for Alfred Hitchcock's *North by Northwest* and later dressed Michael Caine for the cult gangster movie *The Italian Job*.

Tommy Nutter will always be remembered for bringing fashion to the Row with the opening of his first shop, together with Edward Sexton, Nutters of Savile Row, in 1969; with its pop star clientele and open windows it caused a quiet revolution. Splitting with Sexton, Nutter later returned to the row with premises at number 19, from which he continued to dress the rich

and famous, enjoying the patronage of, among many others, shoemaker Manolo Blahnik and musician Elton John. He also dressed Jack Nicholson as the Joker in *Batman* (1989) in that now iconic purple suit, which proved to be his last Hollywood commission before his untimely death in 1992. Following in Nutter's footsteps, several new tailors have now come to the Row, for example, Richard James in 1992 and Ozwald Boateng in 1996. In 2003 the old-established tailors Kilgour appointed Carlo Brandelli as creative director to lead the modernization and rebranding of the firm. All such activity brings to Savile Row a much-needed boost of youthful vitality to carry it forward in the twenty-first century. Tommy Nutter's career was recognized and honoured with a retrospective at London's Fashion and Textiles Museum in Bermondsey that began with a star-studded private view in May 2011.

'Measured Up': the interior of a Savile Row tailors in the 1930s.

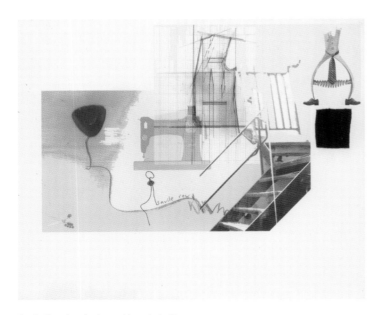

Savile Row-inspired mood boards by Rora Chow (top) and Rebecca Slatter (above), University of Westminster, London.

Portrait of maverick Savile Row tailor Tommy Nutter, 1 February 1973.

Top **Folk/Romany-inspired mood board by Olivia Deane, University of Westminster, London.**

Above **People in traditional folk costumes during the Corpus Christi procession in Lowicz, Poland, in June 2006.**

FOLK   Folk costumes usually reflect a place or a period in history and are very much an expression of that particular location's or era's heritage. Traditional wear is often an indicator of religion, status or social standing, whether for special occasions or in everyday wear, and might also be seen as a backlash against the bland westernization of dress across much of the world – visible signs of pride in their heritage among a region's or country's people. There are still a few places in the world where it is a requirement of law to wear traditional dress, for example Bhutan, as well as some of the Arab states.

Designers are often drawn to the romantic notion of tradition and heritage embodied by folk costume, as well as by its rich decoration, embellishment and motifs.

Above left and right **Vintage folk-inspired fashion garments.**

Above centre **Gucci Autumn/Winter 2008.**

Left **Peasant women in the native dress of Little Russia.**

WORLD

The world's indigenous styles and customs of dress, both ceremonial and functional, have long inspired fashion designers, be it the feather headdresses of the Native Americans, the folk motifs of a Norwegian sweater or a South Asian ikat weave.

In historical terms, there are several factors that have influenced the use of ethnographic elements in design. In the early twentieth century, for example, advances in photography, increased ease of world travel, and the rush of archaeological discoveries in Egypt fed the Art Deco style. As the century wore on, physical access to distant or unfamiliar cultures became easier and developments in mass media allowed images to be shared more efficiently, while recently we have experienced the invention and rise of the Internet. All combined, these components have had a profound impact on the design world in general, and the fashion designer in particular: prior to such developments world research could be based only on the study of detached ethnographic items. Such research is valid, but it is far more rewarding and inspiring to study those items of clothing in situ and in use. Museums and travel remain primary means of research in these areas.

With design research now becoming such a honed discipline in its own right, influences may not be as literal as they once were; take for example Yves Saint Laurent's African-themed show of spring 1967. Nowadays a

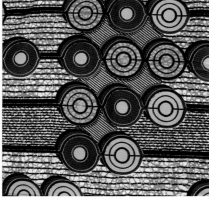

collection often is not simply about one particular place or people, but more likely consists of some fantastical multicultural mash-up; the prints evocative of one culture alongside fabrics and colours from something or somewhere quite different. Junya Watanabe's Spring/Summer 2009 collection featured West African wax textile prints with typically Western denim, which were also seen at Dries Van Noten's Spring/Summer 2010 offering, offset with crisp tailoring. Nicolas Ghesquière's Autumn 2007 collection for Balenciaga featured batik, ikat and kimono prints alongside Peruvian and Mongolian patterns. Galliano delves into all manner of cultures and races, mashing up wildly disparate sources of inspiration in his own inimitable style, while even the sometimes dour Japanese designers do not shy away from brightly coloured African prints and textiles, with Rei Kawakubo of Comme des Garçons using them in Spring/Summer 2008, followed by her protégé Watanabe the following year.

Opposite Men in traditional wax textile robes, Mali.

Above African wax textile-inspired prints seen at Dries Van Noten, Spring/Summer 2010.

Above right West African wax textile swatch.

IKAT TEXTILES 'Ikat' is a word originally from the Indonesian language and is now used in English to describe both the process and the associated cloth. Although a fairly universal technique, with variations seen in places as diverse as Guatemala, India and the Philippines, silk ikat garments were the height of fashion in nineteenth-century Uzbekistan and a symbol of wealth and status. The cloth is made by dyeing the individual silk threads before weaving. The threads are resist-dyed in a process similar to tie-dyeing: threads are tied and bound tightly together, leaving areas of the threads un-dyed. The striking ikat patterns are revealed as the cloth is woven. Double ikat is considered the foremost form of ikat, being the most labour-intensive and requiring the greatest skill to produce; this is a predominantly Indian form, while Japan has its own form called Oshima.

Right An ikat robe from either Bukhara or Karshi in Uzbekistan, Central Asia, dating from the late 19th century.

Below An Indonesian Ikat weaver at work.

Opposite Ikat-inspired dresses at (main image) Gucci, Spring/Summer 2010 and (inset) Balenciaga, Autumn/Winter 2007.

Left African textile research in sketchbook by Rebecca Neilson, University of Westminster, London.

Below West African wax textile swatch.

Bottom A family posing on a riverbank in Mali wearing a variety of wax textile pieces mixed with Western clothing.

AFRICA   Different styles of textile weaving and dyeing proliferate throughout the African continent, including the woven Kente cloth of Ghana, Nigerian Adire tie-dye fabrics and the mud cloth of Mali. Often the processes involved in the making and the particular styles have long and deeply held meanings and significance among the people producing them, as well as great importance for tribal recognition. Wax textiles, typical of West Africa, have made several outings on the catwalk, notably at Junya Watanabe Spring/Summer 2009 and Dries Van Noten Spring/Summer 2010.

Junya Watanabe's mix of Western denim with African textiles from Spring/Summer 2009.

WEST AFRICAN TEXTILES For her Comme des Garçons Spring/Summer 2008 collection Rei Kawakubo produced a print inspired by West African wax textiles and hand-painted African barber's shop signs. Usually brightly painted in domestic house paints, executed by the barber himself or by a local artist or signwriter, and often hanging from a tree or a stall in a market (the African barber's shop can be an ad-hoc set-up), these signs show the melding of traditional African hairdressing and braiding with Western, particularly American, influences. With their naïvely hand-painted pictures showing potential customers the range of available haircuts and braids, the colourful signs can often be dated by the names of the styles – those of personalities and events of global fame: the Nelson Mandela, the Mike Tyson or the Mr T.

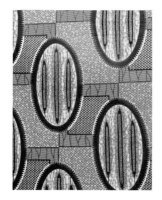

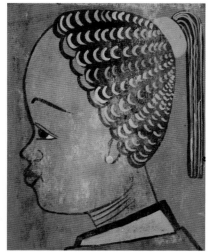

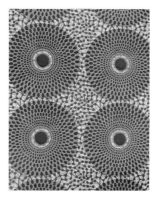

Above right **A traditional African barber's shop sign.**

Left and above left **African wax textile swatches.**

Opposite **Rei Kawakubo's print from her Comme des Garçons Spring/Summer 2008 collection, inspired by African barber's shop signs.**

THE HIMALAYAS Bhutan, Tibet and Nepal, the landlocked countries of the Himalayas between India and China, are rich in traditional costumes and dress, in part thanks to their isolated geographical position in the world. Lack of contact with the outside has helped to stem the Westernization that has happened in so many other places. Bhutanese law stipulates the wearing of national costume at all times outside the home. The women of Bhutan wear a full-length dress, or kira, which is fastened on the shoulder and tied around the waist; underneath this a long-sleeved blouse called a toego is worn. The men wear a gho, a knee-length robe fastened at the waist by a belt known as a kera. Class and social standing determine the colours and decorations embellishing these items of clothing. Scarves and shawls of different colours are also are indicators of status and standing in the community.

Opposite top Tibetan monks dressed in richly decorated silk brocades, black hats and symbols of Tantric Buddhism prepare to perform the Black Hat Dance and chant prayers from sacred texts.

Opposite bottom Three original vintage garments from the Himalayan region, showing intricate embroidered and decorated details.

Right John Galliano's Tibetan mash-up of Autumn/Winter 2004.

Opposite John Galliano's Tibetan
mash-up of Autumn/Winter 2004.

Above Khampa Tibetans performing
in traditional dress during a
summer festival.

Right Details of traditional garments.

Above Present-day women in traditional Peruvian dress carrying children.

Left *Chola Cook* (1900–23), by Edward Carpenter, depicting a young Peruvian woman in traditional dress.

Right Original 1950s vintage Peruvian-inspired dress.

PERU Peru, home of the ancient Inca civilization, lies on the Pacific coast of South America. The Incas were conquered by the Spanish in the sixteenth century. As a result of its multicultural past, the country has a diverse mixture of cultural traditions in art, dress and literature. John Galliano showed several Peruvian-inspired outfits within the Christian Dior haute couture presentation of Autumn/Winter 2005 in Paris.

Above Women in traditional Peruvian dress.

Above right John Galliano's Christian Dior haute couture show for Autumn/Winter 2005 featuring romanticized Peruvian dresses and headgear.

ARCHITECTURE AND FASHION

Fashion, as a design discipline, is moving forward in many of the same ways as architecture; new materials and construction methods are being developed, sought out and utilized; themes and concepts are being shared across the two disciplines. New construction methods in both architecture and fashion allow the creation of novel silhouettes and forms, while other technologies are moving design forward in exciting ways. Both fashion and architectural design have been deconstructed and re-explored in the postmodernist shift of the past thirty years, Rei Kawakubo of Comme des Garçons unleashing deconstruction on the fashion world in the early 1980s, while deconstructivism as a term was applied to architecture a few years later, notably to the works of Frank Gehry and Daniel Libeskind.

Willie Walters of Central Saint Martins has talked about how a student might be inspired 'by a love of modernist brutalist architecture, to love the shapes, the white shapes with the lines of grey grout and the damage on the concrete. And indeed all architectural styles, historical or modern, might be rich in inspiration for the designer or student, whether it be soaring Gothic cathedrals with delicate window tracery of naturalistic forms or the clean lines of the Bauhaus with its slabs of concrete, metal frames and blocks of primary colour.'

Francisco Costa at Calvin Klein, Hussein Chalayan, Maria Cornejo and Raf Simons at Jil Sander are among many modern designers citing modern architecture as a major inspiration, the discipline fitting well with the minimalist aesthetic of these truly modernist designers.

Above **John Curtain School of Medical Research, designed by Lyons Architects, in Canberra, Australia.**

Below **Section through the ground-floor shopfittings and shelves of Neil Barrett's Tokyo flagship store by the architect Zaha Hadid.**

Opposite **Viktor & Rolf, Autumn/ Winter 2003.**

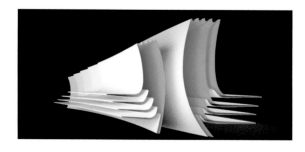

ARCHITECTURE:
DESIGN CASE STUDY

Ju Yeou Hong of Parsons The New School for Design MFA Studies, New York, was inspired by the architecture of New York for her work, as shown on these pages. She writes:

'Inspiration for the research was derived from invention and use of perspective by early Renaissance artists and architects. Study of New York City's skyline, bridges, buildings and streets was an attempt to transform architectural qualities into three-dimensional sartorial forms. Through analysis of the linear forms that I was able to find within architectural pictures, I recreated the shapes and lines using paper origami [mapping them] on to the body forms, where I began to integrate the shapes and experiment with ways to diversify the multiple lines into a sartorial form.'

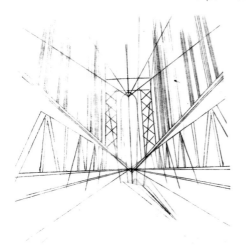

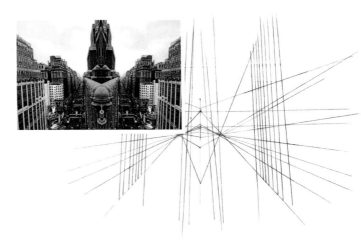

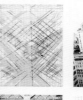

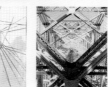

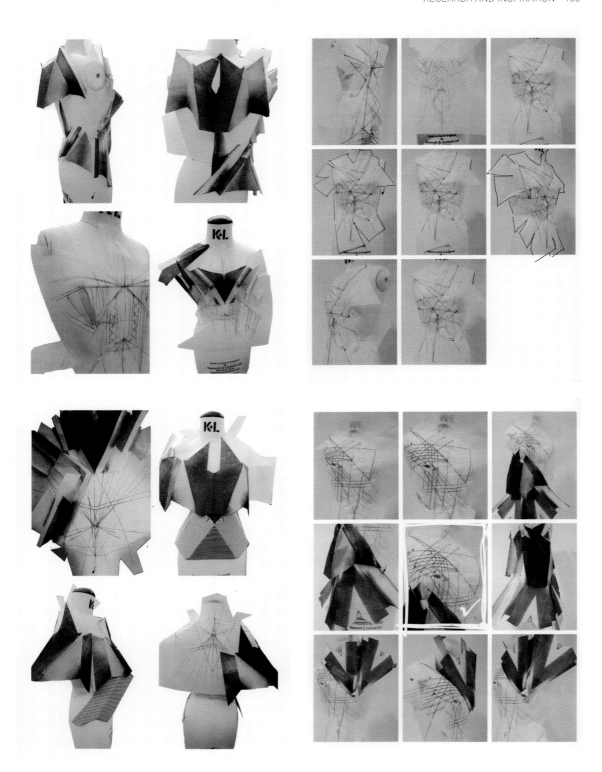

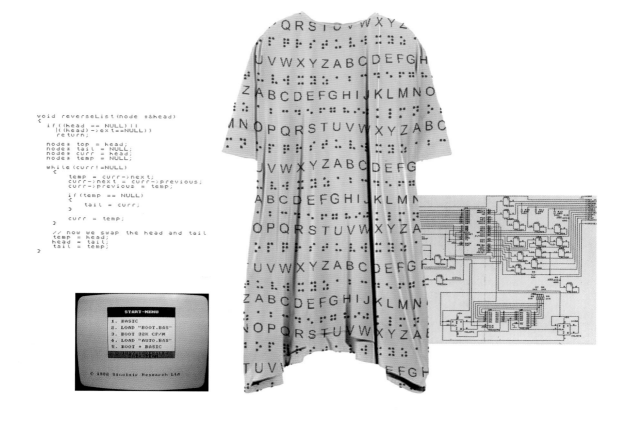

```
void reverseList(node *&head)
{
    if((head == NULL) ||
      |((head)->next==NULL))
        return;

    node* top = head;
    node* tail = NULL;
    node* curr = head;
    node* temp = NULL;

    while (curr!=NULL)
    {
        temp = curr->next;
        curr->next = curr->previous;
        curr->previous = temp;

        if(temp == NULL)
        {
            tail = curr;
        }

        curr = temp;
    }

    // now we swap the head and tail
    temp = head;
    head = tail;
    tail = temp;
}
```

```
START-MENU
1. BASIC
2. LOAD "BOOT.BAS"
3. BOOT 32K CP/M
4. LOAD "AUTO.BAS"
5. BOOT + BASIC

© 1982 Sinclair Research Ltd
```

NATURE AND SCIENCE

Whether analogue or digital, natural and scientific themes continue to inspire today's designers in many different ways, with the results appearing in prints, silhouettes, colours and concepts.

Alexander McQueen's 'Plato's Atlantis' collection of Spring/Summer 2010 was a *tour de force* of technology-meets-nature via the medium of fashion – according to the press release, 'an apocalyptic forecast of the future ecological meltdown of the world'. Strongly tailored and shaped, the clothes were decorated with highly engineered, computer-generated digital prints reminiscent of reptile and fish scales and the shiny, iridescent colours of insects. The show was streamed live via the Internet and huge robotic cameras stalked the catwalk while a film by Nick Knight of a naked Raquel Zimmermann, with snakes writhing across her body, played on the big screen.

Above left and right **Analogue-inspired imagery.**

Above centre **Dress with analogue-inspired print by Richard Nicoll for Stylesight.**

Right **Night sky.**

Below **Jacket with shooting-star print by Marc Newson for G-Star.**

Bottom **Alexander McQueen Spring/ Summer 2010 collection with digital projections.**

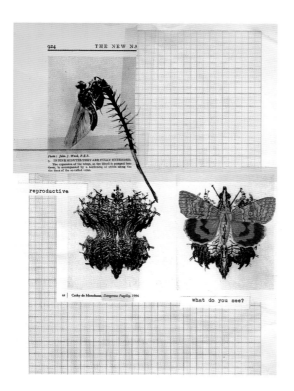

Left and bottom **Insect-inspired mood boards by Tracey Wong, Central Saint Martins, and Harriet De Roeper, Kingston University, London.**

Below **South American green beetle.**

Opposite, left to right **Insect-inspired prints and fabric treatments at Proenza Schouler, Spring/Summer 2010; Versace, Spring/Summer 2010; and Alexander McQueen, Spring/Summer 2010.**

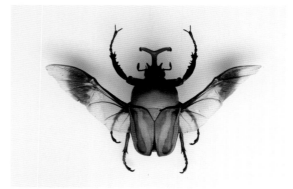

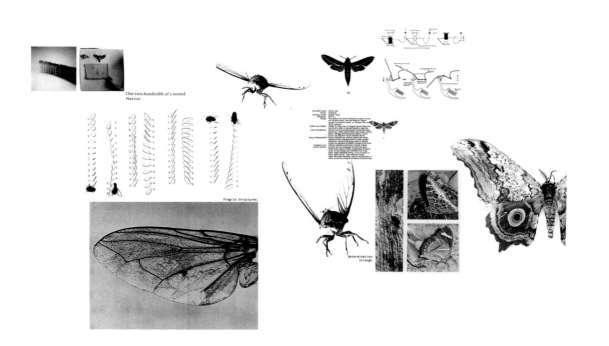

NATURE   Nature, and depictions of natural forms, can be highly inspirational. The shapes and forms of seashells, the wings of a flying insect, or the skeleton of a leaf might inform silhouette, texture or colour for a designer. The collection of images here embodies just one research theme, that of the flying insect, but the designer could just as easily have chosen the forest floor or the deepest ocean bed. Alexander McQueen explored the natural world in the context of global issues of climate change and mass industrialization in 'Natural Dis-tinction, Un-natural Selection' of Spring/Summer 2009 and returned to the nature theme for 'Plato's Atlantis' the following Spring/Summer season (see pages 106–7).

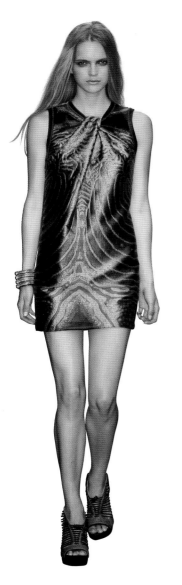

SCIENCE At the cutting edge where science meets fashion is the designer Helen Storey, whose 'Wonderland' project is discussed on the following pages. Storey has also worked on other scientific projects. In one, she and her collaborators have worked out a way to harness the power of photo catalysts: light-sensitive substances that will literally clean the air as you walk. By adding them to fabric softener, clothing can be turned into something environmentally friendly. Storey says: 'We thought we would take a uniform which is universal around the world, so we catalysed jeans.'

Designers are looking increasingly to science and technology for inspiration. Such inspiration might be creative – the never-ending search for the new – or more commercial in application, such as new innovations in fibre and textiles. It might also be entirely visual, such as the collection of images and research from various sources shown here.

The series of images on these pages is based around the theme of black and white contour lines. The images are connected by a common visual thread, reinforcing the effect, magnifying the visual stimulus and enhancing the inherent inspirational qualities, and thereby enabling the viewer to make discernible and useful connections.

'Our ultimate ambition is that we will be able to deliver it into people's laundry so that everyone washing their clothes will purify the air. We think it is going to have an effect on respiratory health. Child asthma is a very serious condition and as a country Britain spends £8 billion a year on respiratory disease.'

Helen Storey

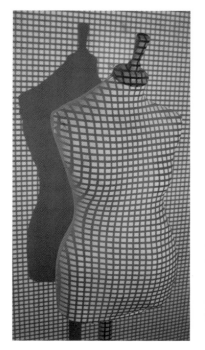 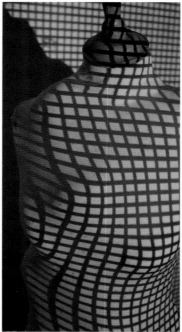 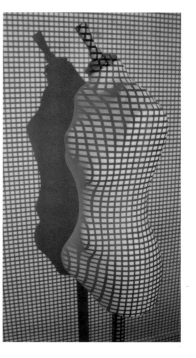

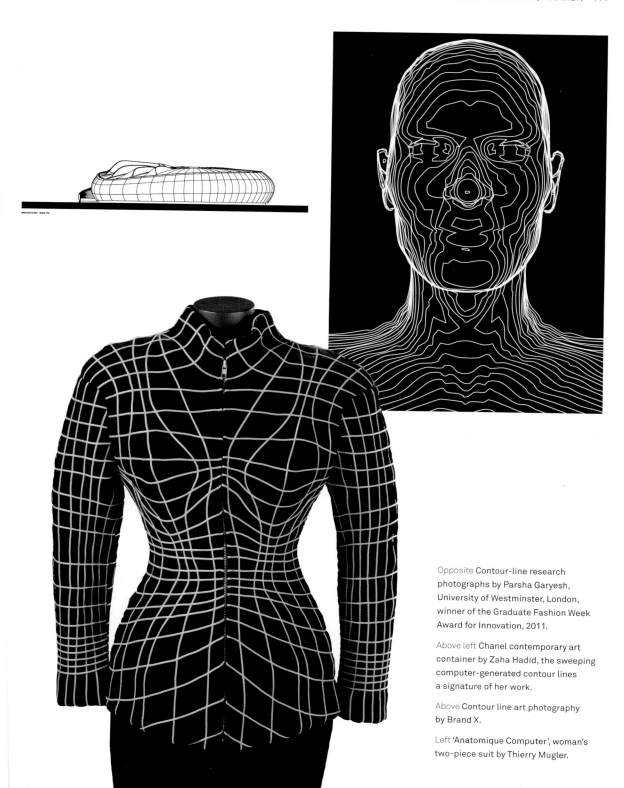

Opposite Contour-line research
photographs by Parsha Garyesh,
University of Westminster, London,
winner of the Graduate Fashion Week
Award for Innovation, 2011.

Above left Chanel contemporary art
container by Zaha Hadid, the sweeping
computer-generated contour lines
a signature of her work.

Above Contour line art photography
by Brand X.

Left 'Anatomique Computer', woman's
two-piece suit by Thierry Mugler.

WONDERLAND

Former fashion designer Helen Storey is at the forefront of collaborations with scientists, and other people outside the fashion sphere, to bring new ideas and thinking into the discipline.

In Storey's words: 'My work widely spans the arts, sciences and new technology fields. I produce projects which illuminate aspects of science and well-being in ways that directly interact with the public, with the broad aim of helping individuals reach their full creative potential. More recently I have begun to focus my creative energy on working in collaboration with other universities to solve global problems.'

The 'Wonderland' project, and in particular the 'Disappearing Dresses' seen here, is the result of a process that began two years ago when Storey began talking to scientist Tony Ryan, a polymer chemist at the University of Sheffield. The pair investigated the possibilities of packaging that would 'know when it was empty and disappear'. The dresses shown here were displayed at a London College of Fashion exhibition in January 2008. Made from textiles that dissolve in water, the dresses are hung from scaffolds and gradually lowered into giant bowls of water.

Using the symbols of the dissolving dress and other works that have arisen as a result of the collaboration, 'Wonderland' shines light on the wider and much greater issues of sustainability and ethical living. Although perhaps vulnerable to cynicism, it is a work that suggests intelligent change through collaboration and experiment.

Ryan and Storey comment: 'We know that if we continue to live the way we are now, the earth will become uninhabitable. Yet we still struggle with the enormity of the thought and so ... it becomes something reported to us in our everyday lives, staining our hearts while frustrating our minds.

'Experience shows that our enormous potential to think the unimaginable is increased most profoundly in collaboration. We deliberately collided our differently trained minds to specifically address some of the planet's greatest problems: lack of drinking water, and non-recyclable plastics. This collision produced a new water purification device and the disappearing plastic bottle, among other ideas.

'We chose dresses to manifest our new approach because we wanted to create something beautifully familiar with which to stimulate an emotional connection. To watch a dress that has taken months to create disappear in a few days seemed to connect directly to that place of unfathomable loss. We hope it may work as a metaphor for our disappearing world.'

Opposite top **Helen Storey at work (left).**

Opposite bottom and below **Images of the 'Wonderland' project.**

DENIM AND WORKWEAR

The origins of the cloth we know today as denim are a matter of some
debate. The name is generally thought to derive from the French town of
Nîmes, where the original 'serge de Nîmes' was made. In his journal for 25
June 1739 a certain Thomas Tye, who worked for London textile merchant
Thomas Hinchliffe, records a cloth known as 'serge denim' – only this denim
was scarlet and he gives no clue as to its actual fibre content. Another,
lighter fabric, originally from Genoa in Italy, was known as 'jean' after the
French 'Gênes' for Genova. By the eighteenth century, 'jean' was made
entirely of indigo-dyed cotton.

Whatever its origin, the fabric and the trousers made from it, originally
intended as hardy workwear for railway workers, farmers, builders and,
of course, cowboys, were to become a central part of the uniform of youth
movements from the 1950s onward. Skinheads, rockers and punks all wore
jeans. From being a signifier of rebellion, jeans were taken up by the young
in general as everyday wear, much in the way that the biker jacket, the
T-shirt and, more latterly, active sportswear have all been.

Above A 1936 drought refugee from
Polk, Missouri, awaiting the opening
of orange-picking season at Porterville,
California, wearing a chambray shirt
and denim dungarees. Photograph
by Dorothea Lange.

Opposite Vintage denim details.

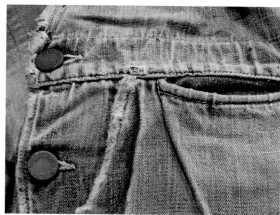

This page Vintage denim and workwear: details.

Opposite Denim and workwear hung out to dry.

DENIM Levi Strauss began selling blue jeans, then known as waist overalls, in California in the mid-nineteenth century, the denim being from a mill in New Hampshire. After adding rivets to strengthen the pockets, an evolution suggested by a wholesale customer, Jacob Davis, Levi's jeans were patented in 1873. They received another patent in 1890 with the addition of the ticket pocket within the front pocket that we still see today. The original headquarters in Battery Street, San Francisco, was destroyed in the great earthquake of 1906 and the company moved to new premises, with a factory on Valencia Street and headquarters on Battery Street. The company rode out the great depression of the 1930s and started producing women's jeans in 1934. The original Levi's 501s had only one back pocket, the second appearing in 1905. Levi's has drawn heavily on its early design heritage for inspiration over the past decade, with a host of new styles based on its unique design vocabulary.

Levi's biggest rivals in the marketplace are Lee. Lee of Kansas was, by 1915, selling approximately 8,500 pairs of its 'Union-All' denim pants and was fast becoming a rival to Levi Strauss; it remains the second largest manufacturer of denim jeans in the United States today.

As denim as a fashion staple grew in popularity it became the job of the designers and fashion companies to reinvent the product to keep up with demand (see pages 120–121).

This page Vintage workwear: details.

Opposite Maynardville, Tennessee.
Photograph by Ben Shahn.

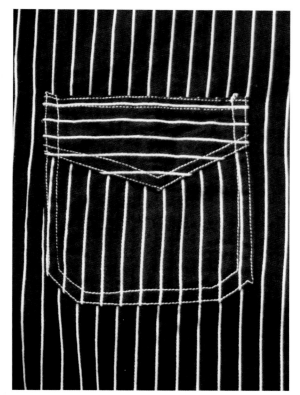

WORKWEAR

Workwear as we know it today is very much an American invention, and the leading workwear brands are almost all based in the United States. Dickies began life as the US Overall Co. in 1918 and was renamed Williamson Dickie; it was a major supplier to US forces during the Second World War, and today is the world's largest maker of workwear. It is a popular brand with the young, notably the skater fraternity.

Osh Kosh B'Gosh, founded in Oshkosh, Wisconsin, in 1895, is probably best known for its ticking striped overalls; it began making them for children at the beginning of the twentieth century, and childrenswear makes up the bulk of the company's business today.

One of the leading brands with a notable crossover from workwear to fashion today is Carhartt. The brand was founded by Hamilton Carhartt in Michigan in 1889, with the motto 'From the mill to millions'. Carhartt expanded during the early part of the twentieth century, eventually having twenty factories and mills throughout North America and Europe. Today its streetwear division has stores in locations all over Europe, and in keeping with the heritage of the brand, many of the garments are still constructed with the triple-stitched seams that have become symbolic of Carhartt.

'I believe that when a man wears an article that I manufacture, his self-respect is increased because he knows that it is made by an honest manufacturer, who is honest with his employees.'

Hamilton Carhartt

DESIGNER DENIM   In the 1960s denim manufacturers began to make different styles of jeans in the fashions of the day, using patchworked, embroidered and decorated denim. Yokes of jeans and collars and pockets of denim jackets were covered with embroidery in a folk or psychedelic style by such companies as Brutus and Falmers. Denim remained a strong fashion staple during the 1970s, and by the 1980s fashion designers such as Gucci, Calvin Klein and Gloria Vanderbilt had started designing and producing own-label jeans.

Bruce Weber and Richard Avedon photographed the early advertising for Calvin Klein Jeans; Avedon art-directed and shot the controversial campaign that featured a fifteen-year-old Brooke Shields.

By the 1990s denim had somewhat fallen out of favour with the youth market, with combat trousers and track pants replacing them as wardrobe staples. However, Levi's bounced back in the late 1990s with a new, more

Main picture **A billboard advertisement for Calvin Klein Jeans in Times Square, New York, 1995.**

This page **Vintage denim garments from the 1960s and 1970s.**

relevant fashion product – 'engineered' jeans, using curved seams and reinvented yet familiar detailing to breathe new life into the cut and feel of their products. By 2000 denim had firmly re-established itself on the fashion map, and it was included in the collections of many designers, where it remains to this day in all its incarnations: bleached, raw, dry (at Céline), distressed (at Watanabe), studded (at Balmain), and embroidered.

SPORTSWEAR

Sportswear, together with its construction, details, aesthetics and styling, has long been an important part of mainstream fashion's vocabulary. With its connotations of youth, vitality and fitness, and its emphasis on the body, it is no surprise that sportswear has become highly influential for both commercial fashion and conceptual runway designers alike.

While true sports performance clothing is based on functionality and fitness for purpose, fashion designers have drawn inspiration from sportswear and its vocabulary to create designs for more conceptual, high-end fashion collections.

Sportswear has become an essential part of the modern wardrobe; trainers and tracksuits are often more readily worn than suits, and high-performance textiles developed for competitive and recreational sports are being integrated into high-end fashion, as are high-tech garment construction methods developed for competitive sportswear. Function and high performance are of primary concern in the design of sportswear and companies invest a considerable amount of time and money into researching performance-enhancing garments, fabrics and footwear.

Sports-inspired fashion may seem a ubiquitous mode of dress these days, but sportswear has only really been worn this way since the early 1980s, with designers such as Bodymap in the UK and Norma Kamali in the United States leading the sportswear-as-fashion revolution.

Nowadays there is nothing more commonplace than a pair of trainers, a hooded jersey top and a pair of tracksuit bottoms; however, individuality is expressed through subtle differences and modifications, colour and, of course, branding.

Above left **An Oxford cox, 1930.**

Far left **American football player and coach Terry Brennan, 1954.**

Left **Major League baseball pitcher Chick Fraser, 1903.**

Opposite top **Two lady tennis players on motorcycles,** c. 1925.

Opposite bottom **Tennis culottes/dress with Art Deco Bakelite buckle, 1920s.**

Recently, fashion designers have integrated many of the technologies used for sportswear manufacturing and fabrication into their designs, often in direct collaboration with sports corporations. At the same time, sportswear itself has become increasingly fashionable and self-aware, frequently looking back at its own design history.

An increasing number of collaborations and hybrids has been seen, with fashion designers such as Yohji Yamamoto and Stella McCartney producing collections in collaboration with sportswear brands; Alexander McQueen designed footwear for Puma; and sports personalities feature in advertising campaigns and even design their own ranges.

From Coco Chanel, who redefined the idea of modernism for the French women from the 1920s onwards, Claire McCardell in 1940s New York, who blazed the trail for other American designers such as Donna Karan, to menswear designer Raf Simons, who has reinterpreted pieces of sportswear into iconic pieces of modern fashion design, designers have long been influenced by the utilitarian ideals of sportswear, its fabrics, detailing and insignia, and continue to be so.

SPORTSWEAR GRAPHICS

Like uniform, sportswear colours and insignia were originally created to satisfy the need for instant recognition, but on the playing field as opposed to the battlefield. Teams and colleges created their own identifying colours and combinations of colours in blocks and stripes, as well as their own trademark fonts and logos.

Arguably the first sportswear logo was that of the Jantzen Diving Girl, designed by Frank and Florenz Clark. Clad in her bright red bathing suit and swimming hat, she first made her appearance in advertisements in 1920, appearing on swimming suits by 1923. Even after several updates, the Diving Girl remains recognizable as a brand logo to this day.

By 1933 Lacoste had begun to produce their then revolutionary tennis shirt with the crocodile logo embroidered on the chest, and the sports logo as branding and brand recognition was born.

Two of today's giants of modern sportswear, Adidas and Puma, were created by two German brothers, Rudolf and Adi Dassler. Rudolf originally registered his new-established company as Ruda, but later changed to Puma. Puma's earliest logo consisted of a leaping cougar, which was registered, along with the company's name, in 1948, and is still used and recognized today. Adi Dassler, his brother, formed the company Adidas; its now world-famous trademark three-stripes branding was bought from a Finnish sports company, Karhu Sports, in 1951. Various court rulings concerning other companies' use of two-, three- and four-stripe designs have decreed that such designs infringe Adidas's three-stripe trademark, effectively barring other manufacturers from using striped decals on their garments; this constitutes a rare case of a decorative garment treatment becoming so famous and ubiquitous that it has become recognized as a logo itself.

In 1971 the American sports company then known as BRS Blue Ribbon Sports decided to launch its own brand, Nike. Carolyn Davidson, a graphic design student at Portland State University, Oregon, was commissioned to create the now iconic Nike 'swoosh', another sportswear graphic logo that, like the Adidas three stripes, the Lacoste crocodile and the Puma cougar, is immediately recognizable the world over.

Brand loyalty is strong among sportswear aficionados; brand identity is fiercely protected, and via lucrative sponsorship deals sporting personalities demonstrate their allegiance to particular companies and brands.

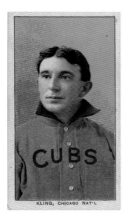

Original baseball cards and vintage American sportswear, showing colour combinations and a variety of fonts and graphics that could provide inspiration for the designer.

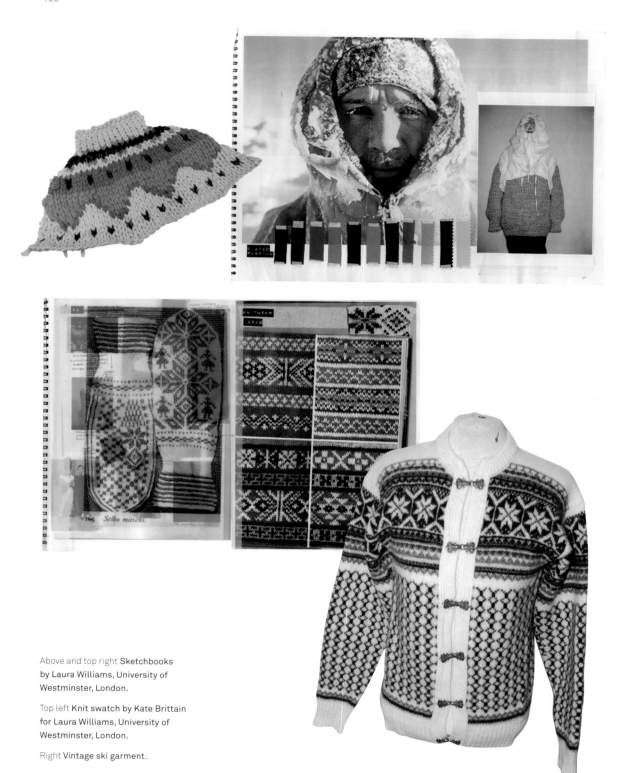

Above and top right Sketchbooks by Laura Williams, University of Westminster, London.

Top left Knit swatch by Kate Brittain for Laura Williams, University of Westminster, London.

Right Vintage ski garment.

SKI WEAR   By selecting a particular sporting discipline, even within a distinct period in time, the designer can find inspiration in numerous different ways: through the colours and combinations of colours, clothing details, pockets, fastenings, and methods of manufacture, as well as from any graphic elements used either on the clothes themselves or in secondary marketing – the images in advertising and editorial. Fonts, typefaces, graphic layout and styles can all evoke a period in time, a national identity or a particular sport or sporting style.

Above **1950s family posing with skis.**

Left **Golden Fleece advertisement.**

ZEITGEIST

Zeitgeist is the spirit of the times. It comprises a wide range of issues, events and things, whether political, environmental, ecological, economic, musical, scientific or technological. It could take in natural disasters, social issues, films, television, pop music or street style.

Sharon Graubard, senior vice president of trend analysis at Stylesight (see pages 38–39), states: 'I am mostly inspired by everyday people on the street, anyone who practises what I call "dressing with intent". People who obviously make choices about colour, proportion, texture, and tell a story with their outfits. … Sometimes these looks are very subtle, but they are often harbingers of what is in the zeitgeist, what will come next, what people are drawn to.'

Katharine Hamnett political statement T-shirt, one of a range she has designed since the 1980s on various issues such as AIDS, nuclear disarmament and, more recently, the anti-Gulf war movement.

Concerning issues of sustainability, Lynda Grose, assistant professor at California College of the Arts, writes: 'It took us a while to realize that the business of fashion and textiles is inherently connected to agriculture. People are more aware of issues nowadays but still at a loss as to what to do about it and how to change their behaviour…. Fashion is immediately available to people across all ages and cultures and touches people every day; it makes sense that fashion would reflect people wanting to do something to help. There are all kinds of other indicators from other disciplines nowadays for mainstream acceptance of sustainability, including people standing in line for the Prius hybrid car, indicating that stepping stones are OK – no one expects to be 100 per cent sustainable.'

Lynda Grose continues: 'The return to craft workshops and facilities is opening up, the pendulum for luxury is swinging back and people are wanting high quality on their own terms, the vertical hierarchies are being eroded, people are becoming reskilled, and ideas for sustainability will pop up from everywhere, from everyday people. Approaches to sustainability in fashion were originally taken piecemeal – organic, recycled, sustainable etc. Nowadays we are more sophisticated and able to diagnose real issues throughout the life cycle and identify appropriate actions that go beyond the stereotypical categories of the 1990s – consumer care, water and labour issues in cotton as well as toxicity.'

On the subject of research and the burgeoning social networking phenomenon, designer and lecturer Andrew Ibi explains how 'Social network media have uncovered many new and previously unseen research topics, so there are still many areas for us to explore and uncover. It's got to be about getting out there and discovering, as the best always will – their need for thirst-quenching will drive them into new areas. The difference is that now these ideas and observations can be instantly uploaded and shared. It will also be about collecting new meanings and directions from topics that have previously been explored. We now have the capacity to piece our history together and make new sense.'

Willie Walters, course director of the fashion BA at Central Saint Martins, notes: 'What's happening in the outside world influences students greatly and the good thing is that that's always changing.'

Some designers are vocal on world issues and often display a political or sociological bent in their work. Examples include Alexander McQueen with his Spring/Summer 2009 'Natural Dis-tinction, Un-natural Selection' collection, Vivienne Westwood's social commentary, both on and off the catwalk, Katharine Hamnett's political statement T-shirts, Moschino's CND logos, Vivienne Tam's Chairman Mao prints, and the Rodarte sisters' sociological comments. Hussein Chalayan is one of many designers interested in science and future technologies, while among designers who conspicuously seek a link with the music scene, Nicola Formichetti at Thierry Mugler stands out, along with Burberry's courting of everyone new and bright in contemporary music, theatre and film.

FILM

Film can influence fashion in numerous ways – in the creation of new trends, by inspiring designers to look back at a period in time and even by giving a glimpse into the future.

Every so often a film comes along that influences contemporary fashion, or conversely a designer is conspicuously influenced by a film from the past that touches a particular chord.

Films with a historical context that have all, in some way, kick-started a trend or inspired a designer for catwalk presentation include *My Fair Lady*, *Out of Africa*, *Goodfellas*, *Barry Lyndon*, *They Shoot Horses, Don't They?*, *Badlands*, *Grey Gardens*, *Bonnie and Clyde*, *Chariots of Fire*, and *The Great Gatsby* (with costumes by a young Ralph Lauren). John Galliano was inspired by Blanche DuBois, a character in Tennessee Williams's 1947 play *A Streetcar Named Desire* (filmed in 1951) for his collection of October 1988, and revisited the source in October 1994 with 'Misia Diva', a collection of twenty-four outfits, again based on the award-winning movie adaptation by Elia Kazan, starring Vivien Leigh and Marlon Brando.

Contemporary films such as *Sex and the City*, *Annie Hall*, *Eyes of Laura Mars*, *Reservoir Dogs*, *Desperately Seeking Susan*, *Saturday Night Fever*, *The Wild One*, *Taxi Driver*, and *Blow Up* are all very much of their period and stand the test of time as stylistic set pieces for designers to look back on and be inspired by. Likewise, the films *Blade Runner*, *The Fifth Element*, *2001: A Space Odyssey*, *Tron*, *The Matrix*, *A Clockwork Orange*, *The Hunger* and *Metropolis*, although from different periods, all feed the designer's creative imagination, presenting as they do a collective aesthetic of futurism.

Opposite Alexander McQueen's Spring/
Summer 2004 offering was inspired
by Sydney Pollack's 1969 movie *They
Shoot Horses, Don't They?* about a
1930s Depression-era dance marathon
in a down-at-heel ballroom on Santa
Monica pier in California.

Below Jane Fonda and Michael Sarrazin
in *They Shoot Horses, Don't They?*

Indeed, Nicolas Ghesquière is quoted as saying he had been watching
The Terminator and *Tron* for his Spring 2007 collection for Balenciaga.

Alexander McQueen was influenced by film many times during his
career. *The Birds*, *Picnic At Hanging Rock*, *The Hunger*, *The Shining*, *Barry
Lyndon*, *The Man Who Knew Too Much*, and *They Shoot Horses, Don't
They?* all became inspirations for his fashion shows and clothes. He even
showed one collection at London's Gainsborough Studios, the studio where
Hitchcock filmed many of his iconic films.

As well as being influenced by films, some designers, notably Jean
Paul Gaultier, have been involved in the designing of clothing for film. He
designed and produced the clothing for Luc Besson's *The Fifth Element*,
Peter Greenaway's *The Cook, the Thief, His Wife and Her Lover*, Jean-Pierre
Jeunet's *The City of Lost Children* and Pedro Almodóvar's *Kika*.

Sharon Graubard of Stylesight (see pages 38–39) comments: 'Every
time I watch an old movie I think, "Wow, a whole collection can be designed
around this", whether it's an old Western, a '60s B movie with Doris Day, or
a '30s black-and-white film noir. There is a wealth of inspiration out there
that will resonate for the moment if interpreted well.' Likewise designer
Paul Smith also identifies movies as a rich resource of inspiration for him,
as does Willie Walters of Central Saint Martins, who added: 'Films are a very
valuable area of research. Personally I love the way Cocteau films are styled
– the whole mood, rather than just the clothes in the film.'

Marc Jacobs was heavily inspired by Jodie Foster in Martin Scorsese's 1976 film *Taxi Driver* for his Spring/Summer 2011 offering, the striped jersey pieces teamed with the floppy wide-brimmed hats being instantly recognizable.

Blade Runner, one of Alexander McQueen's favourite films, was a clear influence on his Autumn/Winter 1998 Givenchy couture collection.

Above **Marc Jacobs Spring/Summer 2011 collection.**

Above right **Jodie Foster in *Taxi Driver*.**

Right **Actress Sean Young in** *Blade Runner*, **directed by Ridley Scott.**

Below **Alexander McQueen's** *Blade Runner*-**inspired collection for Givenchy, 1998.**

STYLE ICONS: THE MUSE

Amanda Harlech, former muse to John Galliano and presently muse to Karl Lagerfeld at Chanel, wrote in the *Financial Times* in 2009: 'I have always avoided analysing what exactly I do at Chanel, feeling that my role is rather like being a high-wire artist without a safety net. The minute you look down at your feet you are likely to fall. In truth, my role is fairly straightforward – to be engaged in the articulation of Lagerfeld's design concept. This involves internalizing his ideas and addressing them without losing myself in them. How would that rounder shoulder feel? Would a higher heel work with a shorter, curving skirt? How do the frilled white shirts balance up against the sugary pastels of the knitwear?'

Historically, muses were the women behind the great designers that inspired them to create. In the early part of the twentieth century muses were women such as Luisa Casati and Iris Apfel, wealthy patrons of the arts and friends of the designers and artists of their day. After the Second World War, among others, famous muses included Audrey Hepburn at Givenchy, Catherine Deneuve at Yves Saint Laurent, Inès de la Fressange at Chanel, Isabella Blow at McQueen and Amanda Harlech at Chanel, all intelligent, often

Below **Jackie Onassis.**

Below right **Alexander McQueen's Autumn/Winter 2005 catwalk presentation, with clear reference to Jackie Onassis during her time as First Lady, including the hair, sunglasses, and late 1950s/early 1960s styling.**

Right Wearing a beret and carrying gloves, film star Marlene Dietrich jauntily strolls along Hollywood Street attired in a grey men's suit, with turtle-neck sweater.

Far right John Galliano Autumn/ Winter 2005 catwalk presentation with Marlene Dietrich as inspiration – a muse he has returned to often.

Below Ladies' suit dating from c. 1960, from the Benenden Collection, Kingston University, London.

beautiful, women in the wings, driving the creative force forward. Today the role has become muddied with the cult of celebrity; pop singers, actresses and models are all held up as muses and style icons. Yet the muse today is just as likely to be the designer herself. The new breed of female designer designs for her friends and for a lifestyle she completely understands, and indeed lives for herself; Phoebe Philo at Céline, Stella McCartney with her eponymous label, and the sisters of Rodarte. Indeed, muses today might even be the very journalists who write about the clothes, such as Anna Wintour, Carine Roitfeld or Emmanuelle Alt. A company such as Mulberry might also, for example, name a handbag after a television presenter.

Rather poetically, John Galliano picked on Maria Lani as a muse for his Spring/Summer 2011 collection, his penultimate ready-to-wear collection as a designer under the Christian Dior umbrella. Lani was an Eastern European actress who arrived in Paris in 1920 and subsequently set about persuading the fashionable artists of the day to paint her portrait ahead of a horror film she told them she was to star in. Fifty portraits were painted in all, by the likes of Henri Matisse, Marc Chagall and Jean Cocteau. Cocteau was to say of her: 'Every time I look away she changes... What a hypnotic force the woman has.' It eventually transpired she was not in fact an actress and there was no movie; she was merely a secretary from Prague. Lani absconded to America with the portraits that had not been sold. It was these fifty portraits that Galliano used as inspiration for the thirty-one looks in his show.

New York straight-ups by Darren Hall.

STREET STYLE

Straight-ups – full-length, part-documentary, part-fashion photographs documenting the clothing style of ordinary people on the street – were pioneered by Terry Jones's *i-D* magazine in the early 1980s. This reportage style has become ubiquitous nowadays, with magazines, books, blogs and websites all adopting this method of recording street-style worldwide. These images are rich in inspiration: the proportions, the combinations of particular garments, the colours, fabrics and textures, and the way they are worn can all inform the designer in their search for the new and edgy.

Many modern design practitioners work from photographic images of clothing on models and mannequins; they layer and manipulate the clothing, maybe collaging it, putting it on in new and different ways and recording the results by sketching or photographing and then working into these images, creating something new and uniquely their own.

Andrew Groves, course leader at the University of Westminster, London, points out: 'One doesn't invent new garments each season but one can reinterpret the way and manner in which they are worn on the body. Layered, distressed, oversized, mix 'n' match, etc. Culturally a square of fabric could be a Hermès scarf, a raver's bandana or a Muslim headcovering; it is all about the manner in which it is worn that gives it meaning and excitement.'

Vintage straight-ups from
i-D magazine.

German-born designer Lutz, who trained at London's Central Saint Martins and now works from Paris, uses the collaging of 'real' clothes on real people as inspiration for his collection. Shown here are images from his Autumn/ Winter 2011 sketchbooks.

Opposite **Straight-ups.**

REAL CLOTHES

As we have seen elsewhere, designers' use of 'real clothes' as research is becoming more prevalent. Maison Martin Margiela's 'Replicas' (see pages 18–19), Lutz's 'cut and shut' collage method (see page 138), and Jens Laugesen's reworking of 'found' garments all fall under this particular umbrella. The method involves taking existing garments and somehow reworking them into the new, by visually collaging them together for inspiration, by dissecting and reworking them, or by making faithful reproductions crediting the original source garments.

Of his reworking of found garments, Danish-born, London-based designer Jens Laugesen said: 'I like to draw inspiration from found garments that will start and nurture the creative research process – working from existing objects liberates the creative outcome, makes it less predictable.'

Regarding the work featured on these pages, he explained: 'For the design process of my first collection, developed while doing my MA at Central Saint Martins, the starting point was a found vintage YSL tuxedo jacket that I started to take apart and modify into proportions I liked. I used the deconstructed jacket as a starting point and it helped me to define the concept. At the same time I started researching intensely in flea markets, assembling a wide range of objects, from a Second World War German nurse's coat to a military cape and jackets. I was fascinated by the utility of the pieces and I found it liberating to be drawn to found objects or garments that spoke to me. At the end I appropriated all these objects and made them all come together to make the first collection, named GROUND ZERO 00, which marked the beginning of my own work.'

Laugesen talked about his work as follows: 'To me the research process is endless. Once you have opened up to find inspiration in anything, then you are liberated, since the ideas will come from the creative research process. For me design is about having a receptive, open mind that is drawn to things and absorbs them like a sponge, and that is able to take the inspiration apart in an analytical manner and to put it together in a more intuitive shape. Research is the starting point that can morph ideas and concepts from various origins into new hybrid shapes. It is important to be open to any potential accidents within the process, and to be able to change the outcome accordingly.

'Through research I will find new ways of observing these objects, and make them evolve. … For me the way I use the research garment is about working them on the stand, to analyse them to take them apart intellectually to find a new form;

'To me the idea of a designer waiting for divine inspiration is over. It is a romantic metaphor of creativity coming from above. To me the inspiration comes directly from the creative process. I don't need to be inspired to work creatively and find that identifying the elements, details, structures or concepts that can start a process, helps contextualize new ideas into the objects/clothes I design. To me it is more about finding new ways of putting together the deconstructed elements into a new hybrid outcome.'

Jens Laugesen

Images of Jens Laugesen's work showing the reworking and subsequent evolution of found garments into new and exciting design concepts.

The front of the jacket conserves the original large proportions of the man's blazer but is worn with unbuttoned front

large top stitching in black...

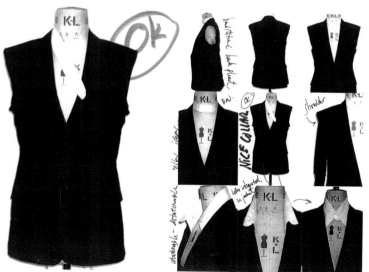

I use the old-school techniques of draping that I learned at Chambre Syndicale de la Couture Parisienne, to find the path between the technique and the creative impulse.

'I think the best visual research is the one that involves a person going out there, a bit like being a "cultural archaeologist", discovering new concepts from various origins and then contextualizing them into a new shape. Photography of the garments on the stand and the body is an important part of my research process, since it allows my eye to see the garment in a disconnected way. It allows me to see the proportions in a more precise manner and to see when it is new and interesting.'

CONCEPTS

Increasingly, these days, designers are looking for new and personal research bases, as research has come to involve much more than just a theme, and thoughts and ideas have become more conceptual and abstract.

A single word might spark a train of thought; a piece of music, a fleeting memory, a found object might all prompt ideas. Over the following pages a selection of different work embodies a variety of themes and suggests the endless potential there is for personal researching and interpretation. For example, a narrative, a story, whether real or imagined, can be utilized to inform the design decision-making process, while a journey might evoke ideas for colour and texture, a found object inspire shapes for pattern cutting, or memories of childhood bring to mind a colour palette. Alternatively, your environment might influence your work, or something as everyday as a cardboard box might be a springboard for a wealth of ideas and design decision-making.

The important thing, as with all research starting points, is not to be slavishly tied to any initial concept. Concepts are springboards for your ideas: remember that whatever form they take, they are merely tools to drive your ideas forward, to take your creative mind to new and exciting places.

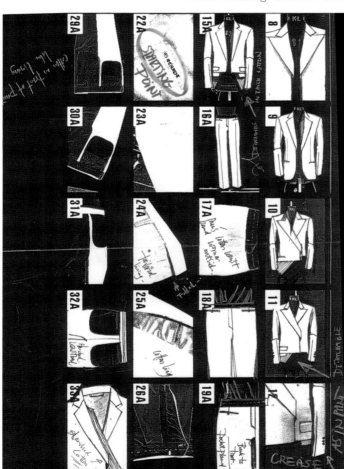

Jens Laugesen approaches his design work, as seen on these pages, from the broad concept of 'real' or 'found' clothing, which he endlessly dissects, re-proportions and reinvents.

NARRATIVE   A narrative, either visual or written, or a combination of both, can be a highly successful means of communicating one's creative ideas. Here, students from Central Saint Martins and Kingston University, London, have taken quotations, responded to written pieces and made visual connections and journeys to inspire their designs.

On this subject, Willie Walters, course director of the fashion BA at Central Saint Martins, says: 'Story building can be wonderful for research: "Here are my grandmother's and grandfather's clothes in Germany"; "Here in the wardrobe are men's and women's clothing, they fell in love and wrapped themselves together."' Walters also notes: 'However, I don't think it's important that the research is visible in the end result, but it is useful for the designer to be able to talk about their research, especially to the press, to convey their ideas. Often just a name of a collection can be totally inspiring. A student this year called her collection "Granouflage", a collection about grannies and camouflage; it was immediately inspiring and understandable as a theme.'

Mood boards with a narrative theme by
Tracey Wong, Central Saint Martins, London.

"From that rubble, from those bit's and pieces, these new life forms are emerging, and we're experiencing their struggle in this very post-human landscape" (Director Shane Acker).

Archaeologists

100 0000 Years after the collapse of industrialisation animal society starts to emerge in the post human landscape. Acting as archaeologists they are left trying to create clothing from a few remaining images left by us, that act as clues to an ideal civilisation. Their child like curiosity leads them to create clothing with no knowledge of how it actually existed 3 dimensionally in our world or how it really created, with no experience of pattern cutting or construction they conduct a number of experiments trying to recreate clothing, the creation's they try might not be right but they try and make them work.

Part's of garments have been dug up and act as sacred artefacts but because of there functional properties they are too valuable not to use, but too sacred to interfere with and so they are adapted to be functional in ways that will not disturb the historical value of the object, for example the garment pieces could be extended by the archaeologists so that pockets can be added for utility and not just cut straight into the garment.

Planet earth is healing itself and some of them work in areas as archaeologists and so adapt clothing to protect them from the planet's harsh environment for example shirts to protect the wearer from the sun and coats made from metallic wall insulation, a material that is light weight and designed to reflect heat inwards thus protecting form extreme cold and extreme heat, as if they ripped it from the walls of the shell of a building and wrapped themselves in it.

Inspired by Shane Acker's animation 9, which tells the story of robot's designed to aid humanity eventually leading to it's demise as they become more and more advanced the machine's are used to enforce a military regime, a twisted form of an ideal society, humanity is eventually wiped out with the robot's lack of logic or empathy , in the last few days of humanity the scientist who created the technology splits his soul in 9 small creation, doll sized being's each developed to take up a certain role and continue life after society. The animation follows the small beings as they adapt the post human landscape to eventually defeat the robot's grip on society and bring about rainfall, allowing plant life to grow once more. Although the characters in my collection might not be children they are small in the grand scheme of the empty planet earth, and very curious.

From this starting point I went on to look at how clothing is adapted at times when the societal norms no longer apply. How civilian clothing is adapted (specifically not military as this already adapted) in times of hardship such as warfare, political protest, flood and nuclear disaster. Horrified by 99% of what I found I also turned to look at the 1960's notion of 'flower power' perhaps a naive ideal in reaction to a time of world-wide political unrest and social change. The idea of a civilisation existing outside the mass 9-5 relying on their emotions and empathy. I wanted the civilisation left uncovering our remains to aim towards the concept of utopia and not warfare which is usually the theme of a post apocalyptic concept, portraying an optimistic outlook on the human race to show the positive of the humanity, we are not machines.

Zac Marshall   The Archaeologists

Out of the corner of my eye
I think i see you standing outside
But its just your shirt
hanging on the washing line
Waving its arm as the wind blows by....

Mood boards with a narrative theme by
Zac Marshall, Kingston University, London.

Mood boards created for a Galliano
project by Jennie Hah, Central Saint
Martins, London.

TRAVEL Fashion designers have long travelled for inspiration, much as the artists of the eighteenth and nineteenth centuries once embarked on the Grand Tour – the stimulus of different cultures, places and visual experiences enlivening the creative mind, providing new references and inspiration for the designer or artist.

Elsa Schiaparelli produced probably the first fashion collections based on ethnic clothes, while Yves Saint Laurent often cited North Africa, where he had a home, as a great source of inspiration for his collections. Contemporary designers constantly travel; Basso & Brooke's Japanese-inspired collection for Autumn/Winter 2009 (see pages 34–35) followed a research trip to Japan, where they took photographs and collected Japanese ephemera to inspire their prints. The late Alexander McQueen visited India before he created his Raj-inspired collection of Autumn/Winter 2008 (see pages 188–189). Paul Smith is a veteran world traveller and keen amateur photographer; examples of his use of his own photographs for his designs can be seen on pages 20–23.

In the images shown here, Molly McCutcheon, a student at the University of Westminster, London, took inspiration from the colours seen on the bullet train on a trip to Japan, which she then built on for her research for her final menswear collection. The results can be seen in the image of her mood wall in the fashion studio at Westminster University. Claire Diederichs of Parsons The New School for Design, on the other hand, looked to the urban qualities of New York for inspiration for colour and form for her work.

Research images by Molly McCutcheon,
University of Westminster, London.

Above Mood board by Claire Diederichs, MFA, Parsons The New School for Design, New York.

Right Mood wall by Molly McCutcheon, University of Westminster, London.

FOUND RESEARCH   Often research material can be happened upon accidentally; a found object might grab the designer's attention. Here, as an example is a work entitled 'Philadelphia Florist', a collection by Shelley Fox inspired by a set of 1937–1939 diaries found at a New York flea market. The diaries provide a rich visual and written record of a Philadelphia florist's business encompassing high-society weddings, funerals, debutante ceremonies and high-profile sports, political and social events.

Celebration, remembrance and the marking of occasions through the symbolism of flowers form the basis of the collection.

The laying out and the dissecting of pattern pieces, from various types of garment, was developed in two-dimensional and three-dimensional form, primarily in paper. These were then transformed into garments, taking the inner workings of the garment, such as facings and finishings, and placing them on the outside as well as the inside.

Other works by Fox involving found research have included the 'Negative Collection' of 2006. 'Found glass photographic slides from eBay began the design inspiration for the new cutting techniques. The otherworldliness of the figures in the glass is haunting,' writes Fox, 'their reversal holding in check any nostalgia for these domestic scenes. Negatives of clothing, sections missing and mismatched belongings bring a new apparition to the forefront. Within the "negatives", sections are highlighted, missing or cut away. Domestic sewing patterns taken from a variety of styles were purchased in East London; they were cut away from their original tissue-paper block and mixed to start creating patterns from scratch. They were layered to create new necklines, using backs as fronts and vice versa, thus creating confusion.'

'Philadelphia Florist' exhibition and research.

IDENTITY   Central Saint Martins graduate Tracey Wong wrote about her work that features on the opposite page: 'The aim was to create a collection based upon a projected muse of my own creation. From this starting point, research imagery, which I feel expresses aspects of this muse, dictates the direction I take, and enables me to realize the mood. The research process itself is quite organic as I prefer not to work in a literal or thematic way; instead I use my research as an expression of mood and a foundation with which I can envisage the type of garments, colour palette and silhouette. My fundamental inspiration for this collection comes from a fascination with the dualistic tensions of women, the transition between youthful naivety and womanly acceptance, and primarily our embodiment of clothing as an extension of oneself.

'As a woman designing for the female body I feel able to apply a more instinctual understanding and appreciation of this concept. Hence, while the garments are not minimal, they are also not designed to dominate the wearer's individuality. Instead they rely on the movement and volume of the body to communicate ideas of modesty and identity.'

Left **Mood boards by Aina Hussein, Parsons The New School for Design, New York.**

Opposite **Mood boards by Tracey Wong, Central Saint Martins, London.**

Through the anticipation of festivity people are permitted to escape for a time

BEYOND A NATURAL STATE

MEMORY An evocation of something past can stir an emotional response; colours, textures, moods can all be evoked. Memories of childhood, people, holidays, schooldays and places can all fire the creative mind and inspire the designer to create. Certain fabrics, their smell, the sound they create when they move: these more abstract concepts are every bit as valid and useful as the more literal forms of inspiration and research.

The work on these pages is by David Gardner of Central Saint Martins, London. Gardner explains the way memory acted as an oblique inspiration for the story underlying his project: 'The world has stood still for many years now and all trace of human life disappeared long ago. Everything since has grown peaceful and silent. Allow your vision to pan on to what was once a little home in the northern streets of Walker, Newcastle, where my small working-class family settled. Mother's weekly wash still hangs on the washing-line in the garden. Now and then, the wind disturbs the statuesque clothes and they come to life again, old dust sprinkles from them and catches like fireworks in the light; old spirits dance once again in their favourite garments. Souls return. Birds, moths and those other

wild creatures have pecked away at the fibres and colour. Dowdy and grey; time has waged a war of beauty over everything that remains and has given us the sights of a ghostly secret garden. Through my collection, I am serving up the archaeological excavation of the Gardner family, using found objects, old photographs, hand-me-downs, fiction and poetry as inspiration. My collection will be an interpretation of the old garments that still hang on the washing line, incorporating the colours and life that have grown naturally around them. I hope to capture a sense of soul, a sense of stillness and silence; I wish my collection to be disturbingly magical.'

Research images by David Gardner,
Central Saint Martins, London.

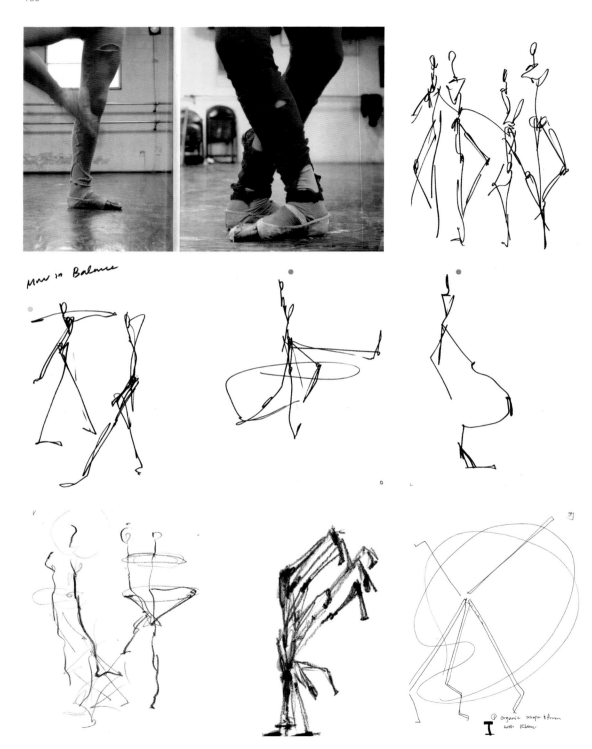

Man in Balance

organic shape & form
with Ribbon

RHYTHM   Themes of rhythm, music and dance were explored and employed in the work featured here by Soojin Kang, Parsons The New School for Design, New York. She describes her project as follows: 'My work is about balance, balance between body movement and movement of music. The inspiration of my design was initiated by observing the body movement of a ballerina and the synchronous classical piano music that flowed harmoniously.

'I began creating my design by sketching line drawings of the ballerina's body movement in the course of time and space. Furthermore, the rhythms and notes of the classical piano music were illustrated graphically in a representational form of patterns. By juxtaposing these two graphical representations, I was able to transpose the lines of movement and patterns of musical notes into my design, determining how the fabric would be cut and how the draping would then form the free-flowing shape in the final garment. By utilizing the method of pulling ribbons through tunnels

in the fabric, I was able to recreate the balanced and dynamic relationship between the movement of ballet and the movement of music. Through the adjustment of the ribbons, the length of the skirt and the fit of the volume would change, enabling the versatility of the design by changing the overall style and the mood it creates. This versatility is my interpretation and my representation of the rhythmical balance between the body movement of ballet and the movement of its surrounding music.'

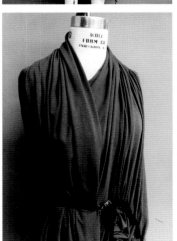

Opposite top left *Legwarmers* by Harvey Edwards.

Opposite and this page **Research images by Soojin Kang, Parsons The New School, New York.**

FORM Inspiration can be drawn from form and structure, both regular and irregular, of extraordinary and everyday objects. Here Zoë Waters, a student at the University of Westminster, London, looked to the humble cardboard box for inspiration for her final degree collection.

During the design process she considered colour, having jersey specially dyed in just the correct 'cardboard' shade; printing, both of box graphics and of the sticky tape used to hold them together; texture, using fine pleating to resemble corrugated cardboard; and then the very construction of the cardboard box. Similar construction techniques were employed for garment construction, the jersey fabric draping and folding of its own volition, but in accordance with the original box construction templates. Hand holes in the original boxes became arm and neck openings, dictating how the box shapes sat on the body, folds became creases, and corners draped softly where they fell on the human form. Familiar packaging graphics decorated their new fluid, fabric counterparts.

Waters commented on her work: '[I started with] the idea of children making dens and hiding, which quickly developed into the idea that children are far more interested in the cardboard box than the toy that was held inside it. This then turned into extensive research into cardboard boxes. I have become obsessed with them, their shape, size, construction, the print on them, address labels, handles, random holes, the tape that holds them together – the list really does go on. After thinking inside and outside the box I hope to have a collection that acts as an ode to the cardboard box, and if not please return to sender.'

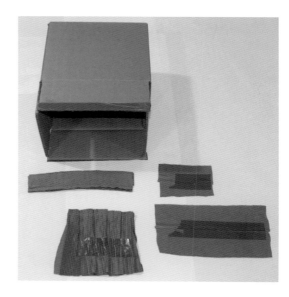

Packaging-inspired research work by
Zoë Waters, University of Westminster,
London.

FABRIC MANIPULATION

The manipulation of fabric for decoration and construction has a long history. It was sometimes born from the desire to decorate: the Elizabethans, for example, developed a fashion for slashing the fabric of their clothes to reveal the linings beneath, pulling the often brightly coloured linings through the slashes. This was a technique that Vivienne Westwood became fond of and on which she based a whole collection, 'Cut and Slash', in 1990; it was to become a signature technique of hers. Other techniques evolved for practicality and utility; for example, quilting – the stitching together of several layers – no doubt developed from a need for warmth and durability. Many techniques, within what we now refer to as fashion, have been honed as clothing styles in the same way; methods of manipulation have been refined as decorative techniques, as shows of skill or status, or as hobbies.

Pleating, although not an entirely new technique, came to the fore with Mariano Fortuny, a Spanish couturier who started work in 1906 and continued until 1946. Fortuny was inspired by the pleating and drapery seen in the sculptures and paintings of classical Greece. His first important

creation was a shift dress named the Delphos dress, made of finely pleated silk weighed down by glass beads. This particular method of pleating remains a secret to this day. The dyeing and printing of the velvets and silks for the pleated dresses were also done using ancient methods.

In the late 1980s Japanese fashion designer Issey Miyake began to experiment with new pleating techniques that would give a sense of flexibility to the wearer, the pleats opening and closing to facilitate movement. In 1993 he created 'Pleats Please', a collection in which the garments were first manufactured and then garment-pleated, as opposed to the traditional method of using pre-pleated fabrics. The garments, cut two to three times larger than normal, are then folded in their paper wrapping and heat-pressed. All manner of pleats are utilized, diagonal, horizontal and vertical, creating new, unexpected and interesting shapes.

Sharon Graubard of Stylesight (see pages 38–39), when talking about fabric and its many forms of manipulation, said: 'Fabric is a key area for research. A fabric will inspire a silhouette: is it drapy, bouncy, stiff or stretchy? Fabric is the paint and clay of fashion. It is so important to understand a fabric's properties, as well as its aesthetics. How does it look, how does it feel, how does it move, how does it tailor?'

Opposite Four Cajun women sewing quilts.

Above Quilted dress by Phoebe Philo for Céline, Spring/Summer 2011.

Above right Quilted dress by Rei Kawakubo for Comme des Garçons, Autumn/Winter 2010.

DRAPE   Draping, the art of design and cutting by fabric manipulation on a three-dimensional form, while by no means new, has become a very popular way of creating new and exciting forms over the past thirty years. It gives the designer the opportunity to create in 3D, something one cannot do with paper and pencil alone. It gives one more of a fully rounded vision than that of the traditional front and back view; side seams might twist or disappear, novel and highly creative forms might appear. Early exponents of this technique were Madeleine Vionnet in the 1920s, followed by Madame Grès in the 1940s, both of whom are cited as influential in their cutting technique by womenswear designer Maria Cornejo (see pages 30–31). A new fashion for 3D modelling was kick-started by the Japanese designers of the early 1980s, Rei Kawakubo and Yohji Yamamoto, although Charles James and Cristóbal Balenciaga were no strangers to the technique some thirty or so years previously. Today, Alber Elbaz of Lanvin is considered one of the new masters of the art, nipping and tucking traditionally couture fabrics such as gazar and mousseline into modern, relevant and new-looking forms.

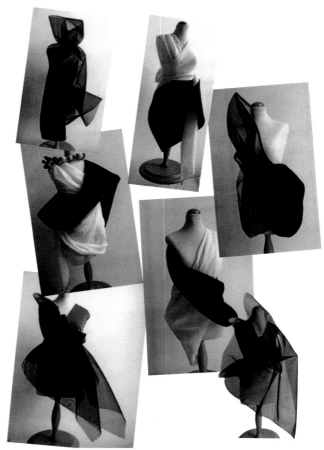

Opposite left **Draped dress by Alber Elbaz for Lanvin, Autumn/Winter 2009.**

Opposite right **Sketchbook with draping work by Catarina Holm, University of Westminster, London.**

Right **Draped dress and headpiece at Junya Watanabe, Autumn/Winter 2008.**

Below **Sketchbook with draping research by Lauren Osborn, University of Westminster, London.**

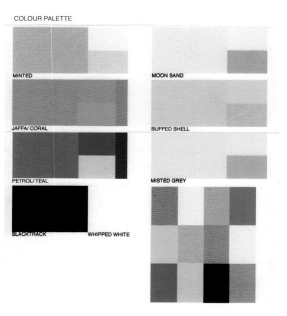

COLOUR PALETTE

MINTED   MOON SAND

JAFFA/ CORAL   BUFFED SHELL

PETROL/ TEAL   MISTED GREY

BLACKTRACK   WHIPPED WHITE

COLOUR

Seasonal fashion is redefined as much by colour as it is by silhouette
or fabric. Designers look everywhere for colour inspiration – from travel to
the environment to art. It might be an image in a photography book, a found
object, or an antique or vintage textile. Newness might come from the
innovative teaming and pairings of colours; newly made-up stripes or
freshly re-coloured prints. The textures derived from modern technologies
in fabric innovation might inspire, as might embellishment or embroidery.
New digital techniques in printing offer new possibilities for colour
and pattern to be displayed. Colour in fashion could also be said to be
influenced by the zeitgeist; a recent downturn in the
world economy saw a shift to more muted colours
such as nudes and greys, while more optimistic times
might herald the return of punchy, bright colours.

**'If one says "red" – the name of a colour – and there are
fifty people listening, it can be expected that there will
be fifty reds in their minds. And one can be sure that all
these reds will be very different.'**

Josef Albers

'Pink is the navy blue of India.'

Diana Vreeland

Opposite **Final colour research images by Tracey Wong, Central Saint Martins, London.**

Far left **Jil Sander by Raf Simons, Spring/Summer 2011.**

Centre **Client presentation colour boxes by Studio M.**

Above **Dries Van Noten, Spring/ Summer 2011.**

MRS ROUSBY

STEREOSCOPIC COY   COPYRIGHT

STRUCTURE

Opposite top left **Ruffled structured piece by Viktor & Rolf, Autumn/Winter 2010.**

Opposite top right **Pleated structured piece by Gareth Pugh, Spring/Summer 2009.**

Opposite bottom left **A Victorian photograph showing actress Mrs Rousby in historical ruffed costume.**

Opposite bottom right **Butterfly dress by Charles James, a wonderfully constructed pleated piece.**

Below **Mood board by Jessica Madden, University of Westminster, London.**

The structural elements that make up fashion and tailoring – pleats, gathers, boning, crinoline, ruffles, padding to the hips or shoulders – can be used to recreate historical exaggerations, such as pannier hips, ruffed necks, corseted waists, or to create something more modern and unconventional. The 1980s saw corsetry, popular in Victorian times and before, come into fashion again, much loved by French designer Jean Paul Gaultier (see pages 182–183), who was responsible for Madonna's stage costumes of corsetry and padding, as well as his corset-laced and structured denim jackets. Comme des Garçons (see pages 176–177) brought us body padding in the seminal 'Body Becomes Dress' collection of 1997, in which clothes were padded with lumps and bumps in unconventional places. Viktor & Rolf's signature play on distortion and form (see pages 192–193) and Alexander McQueen's masterly cutting techniques (see pages 188–189) also show the ways in which structural elements can be employed to striking effect by the skilled designer. Maison Martin Margiela showed its 'Flat' collection for Summer 1998, consisting of pieces constructed so they could lie completely flat; some of the garments could be unzipped to that end (see pages 26–27). Ideas for structure might come to the designer from anywhere, whether from the natural world, the man-made world or clothing history.

3

DESIGNER CASE STUDIES VISUAL REVIEWS

BURBERRY At Burberry, Christopher Bailey was inspired for the Autumn/Winter 2010 collection by the company's aviator heritage: sheepskin-collared aviator jackets were teamed with dresses ruched and strung like parachutes. Burberry has a history of custom-made aviators' gear; in 1937 the company sponsored aviators A. E. Clouston and Betsy Kirby-Green, who, in that year, set a record for the fastest flying time from London to Cape Town.

Bailey has been quoted (on www.style.com) as saying: 'I was thinking of uniforms and cadet girls – but it all started when I looked at an aviator jacket in the archive. Then, as I started designing into it, I realized it could be as versatile as the trench – strong and sexy, masculine and feminine.'

Christopher Bailey and his design team regularly draw on the company's rich past for inspiration. As a company, Burberry kitted out the 1911 South Pole expedition, Shackleton's 1914 Antarctic expedition, early attempts at climbing Everest and many more iconic voyages of exploration and discovery. It has made several types of outer garment its own and as a result has a rich archive and history to feed the brand's particular aesthetic.

A parachute caught by the wind, 19 July 1966, Larkhill, Wiltshire, England.

Left A US Air Force airman in his aviator's gear, including flying jacket and goggles, September 1942. Photograph by Margaret Bourke-White.

Below left Vintage aviator jacket.

Below Aviator-style jacket and parachute-inspired dress at Burberry, Autumn/Winter 2010.

Above **Aircraft wing.**

Opposite **Aeroplane dress at Hussein Chalayan, Spring/Summer 2000.**

HUSSEIN CHALAYAN

Seen as an intellectual among designers, Cypriot-born, Central Saint Martins-trained Hussein Chalayan's themes of the environment, weather, landscape, history, technology and culture have always informed his work.

Among his early design output at Saint Martins were dresses from his college collection 'The Tangent Flows', which had been buried with iron filings in a friend's garden and then dug up again; and dresses made of Tyvek, a paper fabric, printed with airmail envelope striped borders.

These themes of archaeology and travel recur throughout his career. In an interview with Susannah Frankel for *The Independent Magazine* in March 2002, Chalayan said of his Autumn/Winter 1999 'Medea' collection: 'It was like an archaeological dig in a way, but of our own repertoire as well as of references that are more obviously historical, like the Edwardian top of a 1960s dress. After layering it all up we cut it away, which, in itself, I think, creates some new kind of life.'

One of his most iconic offerings is the aeroplane dress from the 'Before Minus Now' Spring/Summer 2000 show, seen here. The dress was operated by a hidden motor and had panels that slid open in the way an aircraft's fins might do during take-off.

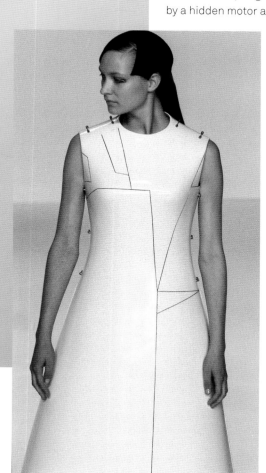

The following season saw his 'After Words' collection. In an interview with Tamsin Blanchard for *The Observer Magazine* in September 2000, Chalayan explained: 'The collection was about leaving your house and hiding your possessions.' Dresses became chair covers and furniture became clothes; a coffee table metamorphosed into a skirt, and at the end of the presentation a chair became a suitcase.

Chalayan has continued to revisit his technological and travel references throughout his career, which has also seen dresses printed with the flight paths of aircraft and remote-controlled resin dresses with moving parts.

CHANEL Credited with the invention of the little black dress, the quilted leather handbag, the tweed suit for women, the first designer perfume and probably the first ever fashion logo, Gabrielle 'Coco' Chanel opened her first business in 1913, a millinery shop in Paris. In the following years her sports- and menswear-inspired, easy-to-wear resort clothing for women would become a huge hit with France's fashionable upper classes. During the 1920s and 1930s, Chanel revolutionized the way in which fashionable women dressed.

Chanel closed the business with the outbreak of war in 1939, not reopening again until 1953, when she met with stiff competition from new male couturiers such as Christian Dior. Despite this the business survived until 1971 when, aged eighty-seven, Chanel died in Paris. The business remained in private hands, as it does to this day – those of Alain and Gerard Wertheimer, grandsons of Pierre Wertheimer, the original financial backer of Chanel's No. 5 perfume. In 1983 Karl Lagerfeld, previously designer for

the House of Chloé, was appointed as creative director and the business set about reinventing itself as a fashion force, based on its firm stylistic roots and visual heritage. Chanel's signature knobbly tweeds, the strings of pearls and camellias, the quilted handbags on gold chains and the braiding are all deftly reworked for the luxury fashion market, season after season. On the opposite page we see these motifs adapted for the Inuit-themed show of Autumn/Winter 2010.

Opposite left **Signature tweed two-piece suit from Chanel's 1969 collection.**

Opposite right **Karl Lagerfeld.**

Above left **Portrait of Inuits Micoc and her son Tootac,** *c.* 1769.

Above **Inuit-inspired outfit by Karl Lagerfeld for Chanel, Autumn/ Winter 2010.**

Left **Eskimo group photographed by the Gerhard Sisters, 1904.**

COMME DES GARÇONS Rei Kawakubo's inspirations for her Comme des Garçons label (see also pages 40–41) have been far-reaching and often obscure; she described her Spring 2004 collection as being about 'designing from shapeless, abstract, intangible forms, not taking into account the body'. She constantly plays with silhouettes of the Victorian and Edwardian periods, never tires of the sombre severity of black, and continually blurs the boundaries between the masculine and the feminine. The cutting is always extraordinary, as often are the fabrics and combinations of fabrics. Frequently it is these very juxtapositions that give strength and newness to her collections; of Spring/Summer 2005 she said: 'I thought about the power of the motorbike – the machine itself – and the strength of a ballet dancer's arms.' She continues to push fashion forward, a free thinker and visionary. The catwalk image here is from her Autumn/Winter collection of 2005: a Victorian bridal-inspired collection, mostly in white, with antique lace and delicate pleating, the fabrics those of the bride – satins, tulles and lace. The soundtrack was one of church organ music interspersed with the sounds of different marriage celebrations from around the globe.

Opposite, clockwise from top left
A girl wearing a lace dress for her First Communion; vintage broderie anglaise dress; wedding portrait of Helen Taft Manning; vintage broderie anglaise dress.

Left Comme des Garçons' Autumn/ Winter 2005 wedding dress-inspired collection.

CHRISTIAN DIOR On 14 October 1996, John Galliano replaced Italian designer Gianfranco Ferré at Christian Dior. His first couture show for Dior, on 20 January 1997, coincided with the label's fiftieth anniversary. Galliano has said that his love of theatre and femininity is central to his creations: 'My role is to seduce.'

In Galliano's presentation for Christian Dior Couture in Spring/Summer 2007, *Madama Butterfly*, the Puccini opera set in Japan, met origami, the Japanese art of paper folding. However, it was not paper but rather fabric that was folded and exquisitely cut and sewn into origami forms. The Japanese theme was further amplified by intricate Japanese cherry blossom embroidery and geisha girl make-up. Other Dior shows, the most lavish being the haute couture presentations, have had such diverse themes as Cukor's 1939 film *The Women*, top model Lisa Fonssagrives, and the French Revolution of 1789. The final Christian Dior show with Galliano as designer went ahead on 4 March 2011.

Opposite Geraldine Farrar as Madam Butterfly.

Top Japanese origami.

Above Poster by Leopoldo Metlicovitz for a production of Puccini's opera *Madama Butterfly*, 1900.

Left Galliano's 'Madama Butterfly' collection for Christian Dior Haute Couture, Spring/Summer 2007, with origami-inspired cutting and Japanese-inspired embroidery.

JOHN GALLIANO Born in Gibraltar, John Galliano moved with his family to London at the age of six. Later he attended Saint Martins School of Art (now Central Saint Martins), graduating in 1984. He was awarded British Designer of the Year in 1987, 1994 and 1995, while in 1997, he shared the award with Alexander McQueen, his successor at the House of Givenchy.

His graduation collection of 1984, shown in the Floral Hall in London's Covent Garden, was inspired by the French Revolution and entitled *Les Incroyables*; it was bought by and sold in the London fashion boutique Browns. Galliano began his own label and met future collaborators Amanda Harlech, *Harpers and Queen* fashion stylist, and fellow Saint Martins-trained Stephen Jones, the milliner (see pages 26–27).

Galliano relocated to Paris in 1988, in search of financial backing and a strong client base. With the help of American *Vogue* editor-in-chief Anna Wintour and European correspondent at *Vanity Fair* André Leon Talley, Galliano was introduced to financial backers and also received the society endorsement needed to give him credibility in Paris. His first show, important in the development of John Galliano as a fashion house, was in 1989 as part of Paris Fashion Week. Supermodels waived their usual fees, and financial backing along with the use of an unoccupied Parisian mansion as a temporary studio and suitably theatrical venue for the show allowed Galliano to produce a collection of seventeen black outfits with a 1940s theme. Galliano relaunched himself and his fashion house on the worldwide fashion scene.

In July 1995, he was appointed as the designer of Givenchy, and in 1996 he moved to Christian Dior (see pages 178–179), where he remained until March 2011. Between his own label and Dior, Galliano produced at least six collections a year, naming those collections after his visual research inspiration and often using that stimulus to create lavish sets and staging for his presentations. His influences have remained widespread but characteristically his, in particular the stars of the silent screen, ballet and the theatre. Glamorous women and movie stars of the 1940s, the art of the Surrealists and fabulous indigenous costume from all corners of the globe are often mashed up and thrown into the mix in his inimitable style.

Main image **Souvenir Russian nesting dolls.**

Left **Russian-doll-inspired outfit from John Galliano's Autumn/Winter 2009 collection.**

JEAN PAUL GAULTIER   Jean Paul Gaultier employed all his signature themes in this look from his couture show from Spring/Summer 2008: the matelot stripes, the tattoo prints, the military tailoring – the whole nautical flavour so associated with the design house.

Gaultier never received formal training as a designer; Pierre Cardin hired him as an assistant in 1970 and after this he worked with Jean Patou. His first eponymous collection was shown in 1976.

Many of Gaultier's collections have been based on streetwear, particularly focusing on popular culture; conversely his haute couture collections are more likely to draw inspiration from the world's many disparate cultures, from Hasidic Judaism through tribal Africa to imperial India.

Creative high points of his career include the 1985 introduction of skirts for men; the 1988 label Junior Gaultier, a diffusion line aimed at the youth market with a flavour combining streetwear and nautical, which went on to influence most of his work in both clothes and promotional material as well as perfumes; and Madonna's stage costumes during the 1990s, including the famous cone bra for her 1990 Blond Ambition tour and the costumes for her 2006 Confessions tour.

Gaultier has been ground-breaking in his use of unconventional models for the catwalk, featuring androgynous models, older men, plus-size women and models with tattoos and piercings.

An outfit from Gaultier's Couture Spring/Summer 2008 collection, which referenced his favourite nautical themes, here seen in the shimmering metallic mermaid's-tail skirt with sailor-striped top, beautiful tattoo-printed gloves and exquisitely tailored cashmere overcoat, with the model's hair in tendrils, reminiscent of seaweed.

Right A sailor being tattooed by a shipmate aboard the USS *New Jersey*.

Below right Mermaid swimming in a tank; detail from turn-of-the-century circus poster.

Below Pierre Savorgiran Brazza (1852–1905), French sailor and explorer of the Congo, with two sailors.

MARC JACOBS

Marc Jacobs was born in New York, where he attended Parsons The New School for Design. During his time at Parsons, Jacobs won the Perry Ellis Gold Thimble and the Design Student of the Year Award, both in 1984. Following his studies, Jacobs began as designer at Perry Ellis after the death of Ellis. In 1986 he designed his first collection with his own Marc Jacobs label and in 1987 he was awarded the Council of Fashion Designers of America (CFDA) Perry Ellis Award for New Fashion Talent. In 1992, they again honoured Jacobs, this time with the Women's Designer of the Year Award; that was also the year he showed his 'Grunge' collection for Perry Ellis, which attracted the attention of the fashion press but also resulted in his dismissal. In 1994 he showed his first collection of menswear.

In 1997, Jacobs was appointed creative director of luxury French fashion house Louis Vuitton, producing the company's first ready-to-wear line. At Louis Vuitton, he has collaborated with many artists for his collections, including Stephen Sprouse, Takashi Murakami and Richard Prince.

Many of his Marc Jacobs and Marc collections are influenced by the fashions of past decades in history. Any era from the Victorian period through to the 1980s might be referenced, as might the work of the great designers of the past in subtle homages to, for example, Yves Saint Laurent or Missoni. His work could also sometimes include immediately recognizable cultural and film references.

Opposite top left Two elderly women sharecroppers sitting on the porch of a log cabin. Photograph by Margaret Bourke-White.

Opposite top right 'Americana' by Marc Jacobs, Spring/Summer 2009.

Opposite bottom left A girl trying on an extra-large straw hat. Photograph by Genevieve Naylor.

Opposite bottom right Antique American silk blouse, c. 1890.

Below Young residents at Amite City, Louisiana. Photograph by Ben Shahn.

RALPH LAUREN Lauren was born Ralph Lifshitz in the Bronx, New York; he changed his name to Lauren at the age of sixteen, along with his brother Jerry. At his high school Lauren is remembered by his former classmates for selling ties to his fellow students. He never studied fashion, but went to the Baruch School of Business and Civic Administration, where he studied business. From 1962 to 1964 he served in the United States Army and in December 1964, he married Ricky Anne Low-Beer in New York.

Lauren worked for Brooks Brothers as a salesman and in 1967, with the financial backing of Norman Hilton, he opened a store where he designed and sold neckties under the label Polo – a name he would later purchase from Hilton.

In 1972 Ralph Lauren released the short-sleeved piqué casual shirt with the polo player logo; it came in twenty-four colours, and soon became a fashion classic. In the following years he built his business on the reinvention of the classics, bringing a real sense of Britishness, the upper classes and the English countryside to American fashion. In his fortieth anniversary show Ralph Lauren revisited all his passions; he has said: 'I drew upon everything I ever loved, and that was it.' After a long and successful career he rounded up all the quintessentially British motifs he

is so fond of: *My Fair Lady* dresses based on Cecil Beaton's costumes for Audrey Hepburn in the classic film; equestrian themes of jodhpurs and riding jackets, jockey silks and horsey prints; the London City gent's garb of bowler hats and dark suits complete with furled umbrellas; and long dresses in what Suzy Menkes, in her *International Herald Tribune* review of the show on 9 September 2007, described as 'floral English wallpaper prints'.

UNE GROSSE COTE

Left *Men with Jockey* by Pierre Mourgue.

Opposite **Ralph Lauren** Spring/Summer 2008 collection, with jockey- and city gent-inspired outfits.

ALEXANDER MCQUEEN

Lee Alexander McQueen left school aged sixteen in 1985, with just one O-level in art. He worked for a period in Savile Row, where he learned the tailoring skills for which his work would later be renowned. After a spell working in Italy, in 1994 he enrolled on the MA course at Central Saint Martins, and on graduation his collection was bought by Isabella Blow, then a stylist at *Vogue*.

McQueen's early collections earned him his reputation for shock tactics and controversy; designing trousers so low-rise they were named 'bumsters' as well as presenting his 'Highland Rape' collection of 1995. *The Hunger*, a vampire film-inspired collection, followed; and then 'Dante', based on Dante's *Inferno*. Artist and photographer Hans Bellmer inspired the next collection, Summer 1997's 'La Poupée'. Subsequent collections had themes as diverse as Joan of Arc and the Yoruba people of West Africa. McQueen became known for his lavish catwalk productions, often under the supervision of art director Simon Costin; it snowed and rained on his catwalks; we saw a shipwreck, a forest, a human chess game and, in Autumn 1998, robotic arms spraying paint on to a white dress worn by supermodel Shalom Harlow. Double amputee Aimee Mullins strode down the catwalk on custom-made limbs, and in his 2006 show 'Widows of Culloden', the audience witnessed a ghostly life-sized hologram of supermodel Kate Moss.

McQueen has been credited with bringing drama and extravagance to the catwalk. He was inventive in his use of technology and innovation to bring modernity to traditional themes, and his shows shocked, surprised and delighted audiences.

Opposite A photograph taken at the Silver Jubilee of Maharaja Jagatjit Singh of Kapurthala, India, portraying local rulers, c. 1920s.

Below Alexander McQueen's Raj-inspired collection from Autumn/ Winter 2008.

Below right A young Queen Victoria, portrayed in 1842.

Bottom right Traditional Indian wedding sari.

In December 2000 the Gucci Group acquired fifty-one per cent of his company and McQueen became creative director. Expansion saw the opening of stores in London, Milan and New York, and the launch of perfumes Kingdom and My Queen. In 2005, McQueen began collaborating with Puma to create a range of trainers for the sports brand, and in 2006 McQ was launched, a younger, more affordable diffusion line for both sexes.

Lee Alexander McQueen died in February 2010. The company continues, headed by former design assistant Sarah Burton and continuing to draw on the rich legacy of research left behind: a legacy of film references, literary references, family and historical references, as well as those of the work of artists and photographers that inspired the designer to create.

'The Giant fell headlong into the garden.' Illustration by Margaret W. Tarrant (1888–1959).

PRADA Prada was founded in Milan in 1913 by Mario Prada and his brother Martino, but it was Miuccia Prada, who joined the company in 1970, who eventually bought the company to the fashion fore by releasing her first collection of backpacks and tote bags in 1979. They were made out of the tough black nylon that her grandfather had previously utilized as the coverings for steamer trunks. By 1984 the black nylon totes and rucksacks had become a worldwide fashion hit.

Miuccia Prada continued to grow the company; after she launched its eponymous women's ready-to-wear collection in 1989, Prada's popularity and reputation increased enormously among the fashion cognoscenti. Its ultra-modern aesthetic teamed with new and unusual colour and fabric combinations appealed enormously to the fashion-conscious consumer, as did their more low-key, but still high-luxury, branding.

Miuccia Prada is renowned for the strangeness and obliqueness of any inspiration and references for her collections, often offering waiting journalists one-line soundbites such as 'It's primitive', 'Something simple but strange', or 'I'm tired of being so sweet'.

Featured here is one of her perhaps more visually tangible collections; that of Spring/Summer 2008. The vaguely 1970s Art Nouveau revival psychedelic prints of fairies and wood nymphs adorn silk tunics and trousers – the stuff of children's fables meets prog-rock album covers.

Sarah Mower, on www.style.com, dubbed Miuccia Prada 'fashion's most restless creative force'.

Above *Psilocybe cyanescens*, a potent psychedelic mushroom.

Left Miuccia Prada's Spring/Summer 2008 collection with naturalistic fairy-tale prints.

VIKTOR & ROLF   Viktor Horsting and Rolf Snoeren attended the Arnhem Academy of Art and Design in the Netherlands and began working together on graduation, relocating to Paris in 1993 to launch their careers. Their first collection, the award-winning 'Hyères' of 1993, was based on themes of reconstruction, layering and distortion. They subsequently showed four collections in art spaces, after which, in the spring of 1998, they presented their first haute couture collection. They made a return to ready-to-wear with 'Stars and Stripes' for Autumn/Winter 2000. Their menswear line Monsieur was added in the autumn of 2003.

Viktor & Rolf, like Comme des Garçons, Lanvin and Karl Lagerfeld, have collaborated with Swedish high street chain H&M. Their recent collections have included upside-down dresses, shown with played-backwards music; ball gowns with seemingly impossible shot-through holes; and in one case, a lone model, on a revolving platform, layered up in lots of looks like a Russian doll. Their fifteen-year retrospective in 2008, at London's Barbican Art Gallery, featured a giant doll's house with more than fifty dolls, each wearing a miniature version of a past Viktor & Rolf look.

Right **Isamu Noguchi's** *Red Cube* located in front of the Marine Midland building on Broadway, New York.

Opposite **Viktor & Rolf, Spring/Summer 2010.**

JUNYA WATANABE

Japanese designer Junya Watanabe, a 1984 graduate of Japan's Bunka Fashion College and protégé of Rei Kawakubo of Comme des Garçons, began to show under his own name in 1992. As a designer he is able to draw successfully from a small research base, reworking a black down-filled puffa jacket into wonderful dresses, an African textile into draped and intricately cut garments, or a military flying suit into tailored pieces, trousers and trench coats. He reinterprets everything in many different ways but still deftly manages to keep each piece fresh and exciting and true to the original research concept. Each show is born of one or two usually narrow areas of research and deftly spun out into forty or fifty outfits based on that initial visual stimulus.

In his Autumn/Winter 2006 show Watanabe chose the combat-green flying suit and associated military wear as his primary research. The suits were endlessly reworked into different types of garment: shirts, trousers, coats and dresses. These forty-four looks based on essentially one garment were a master class in the art of reinvention based on thorough and highly focused research.

The look held strong for several reasons: the authenticity of colour and fabric, the only deviation being a lace (but even this was dyed to precisely the right military green), but most of all the instantly recognizable details. There were webbing belts, zips and map pockets. The bound inner edges came outside and the multiple rows of stitching were evident; the language of the flying suit was present and correct in every piece.

Opposite **Junya Watanabe's Autumn/ Winter 2006 collection based on flying jackets.**

This page **Vintage RAF flying jacket.**

VIVIENNE WESTWOOD Always a designer with the ability to divide opinion and shock, Vivienne Westwood was born Vivienne Isabel Swire in 1941 in Derbyshire. She moved to London in 1957 and attended Harrow School of Art, now the University of Westminster, though did not graduate. Eight years later she met Malcolm McLaren, and in 1971 the pair opened their first shop, named Let It Rock, at 430 King's Road. A year later the shop was redesigned and renamed Too Fast To Live, Too Young To Die, and another revamp a year later saw it changed to SEX. In 1976 the shop – now named Seditionaries – became the spiritual home of the new youth movement known as punk. McLaren managed the newly formed punk band the Sex Pistols, who wore many of the designs created by Westwood and McLaren and sold through their boutique. Following the peak of the punk movement in 1980, the shop became known as World's End and Westwood and McLaren showed their seminal 'Pirates' collection for that Autumn/Winter season, inspired by historical pirate costume, both real and the stuff of storybook and legend, including Madras cotton stripes, tassels, tricorn hats and the now-trademark 'squiggle' prints. Collections following this included 'Savage' in Spring 1982, 'Buffalo' in Autumn/Winter 1982–83 and 'Punkature' in Spring 1983. That same year they opened a second shop in St Christopher's Place, London, called Nostalgia of Mud. 'Hypnos', the collection for Spring/Summer 1984, in a move from London, was shown in Milan.

Westwood's first, and influential, menswear collection, 'Cut and Slash', was shown at Pitti Uomo in Florence in 1990, and that same year, the first eponymous Vivienne Westwood shop opened at number 6 Davies Street, London, selling the Red Label collection. In 1999, the Red Label collection was launched in the United States, coinciding with the opening of the first Westwood shop in New York. In 2004 the Victoria and Albert Museum, London, staged a major retrospective of the work of Vivienne Westwood.

Concerning her 'Prince Charming' collection of Autumn/Winter 2010, Westwood has written:

'The way I most often start a collection is by doing something practical. Looking at the first jacket, still on the stand, something about the shoulders and the proportion reminded me of a principal boy in a pantomime. I decided to have as a working title the idea of fairy tales and I didn't know whether to call the collection "Sleeping Beauty" or "Prince Charming". Prince Charming won. The first exit of the show is a coat developed from this jacket. This character is Prince Charming, as you may guess from his blue tights. You will see Hansel and Gretel and the kind of people you could meet in the Black Forest of Grimm's Fairy Tales.

'The traditional folklore fairy tale is very important for children as there is deep psychology in it. Fairy tales are about dealing with danger, injustice and terrible morality. They help children to become independent and mature by facing up to all kinds of things on an imaginative level.

Opposite **Vivienne Westwood.**

Above *Helen of Troy* by Dante Gabriel Rossetti.

The great thing is the hero always wins in the end, even when he is a simpleton or an un-empowered person. A little girl of about five was really fascinated by the story of Cinderella. One day she said to her astonished mother, "You needn't treat me so badly just because I am the most beautiful member of the family." A little boy said to his father who was reading him *Jack and the Beanstalk*, "There aren't any giants today, are there?" Before the father could reply he said, "But there are grown-ups."

'The context of everything I do at the moment is to do with climate change. Like everyone who has woken up to the fact that we are an endangered species I try to do something about it. And I wish to understand the world.

'Human history is so incredible. We've looked at the world in different ways so many times and we adjust our opinions every day. The world changes and we change. Every epoch sees a new world. Life is rich and cruel and we, the lucky ones are having a great adventure.

'There is a Renaissance painting in the National Gallery by Jan Gossaert of the Epiphany; the holy family, angels and the three wise men and their retinues: I used it as a test. Every one of my designs would fit in amongst the rich panoply. Travellers from the east have arrived here following their star; there is a page boy whose job it is to hold the train of his master's cloak. What a different life he led from us. The world has always been different.'

Left *Mrs Henry Beaufoy* by Thomas Gainsborough.

Opposite Vivienne Westwood's Autumn/ Winter 2010 collection inspired by historical dress.

YOHJI YAMAMOTO Born in Tokyo in 1943, Yohji Yamamoto first came to prominence on the European fashion scene after being invited, by the Chambre Syndicale de la Couture Parisienne, to show in Paris in 1981, along with fellow Japanese designer Rei Kawakubo and her label Comme des Garçons (see pages 40–41 and 176–177). His black, menswear-inspired womenswear shocked and excited the fashion cognoscenti in equal measure. His favoured monochrome black, along with his eschewing of any excess of decoration or adornment, is described by the designer as 'focusing the eye on the cut'.

In the 1989 Wim Wenders documentary on Yamamoto, *Notebook on Cities and Clothes*, the designer describes how he looks for inspiration at the photographic portraits of German society by German photographer August Sanders in the book *People of the 20th Century* – a book, incidentally, also named by Rei Kawakubo as a source of research material. Other sources of inspiration quoted were the black mourning clothes of his mother, his father having been killed in the war: 'She wore nothing but black mourning clothes and I would watch as the hem of her skirt fluttered.' Here was a new breed of designer concerned with totally modern concepts, those of movement and

Left Yohji Yamamoto's Spring/Summer 2008 collection, with Victorian-inspired ruffle skirt and mannish tailoring.

Below **Ruffle skirt, 1861.**

innovative cutting techniques, as well as with the blurring of the lines between long-held traditions of mens- and womenswear.

In an interview with Susannah Frankel in *The Independent* of November 2010, Yamamoto says, ahead of his major retrospective at the Victoria and Albert Museum in London: 'I think the most important thing is that I have continued to do the same thing, to send out the same message, to remind people I am still here. Then people who are so enamoured with the market might think, "Yohji always does something creative, he doesn't follow fashion or the trends, he has never followed fashion or the trends". Maybe I can be like that, maybe that's enough. To keep on going by myself, for myself, and hope that makes a difference to the people who doubt.'

Top **Drawings by Yohji Yamamoto.**

Above **Portrait of Yohji Yamamoto by Mark C. O'Flaherty.**

BIBLIOGRAPHY

Behrens, Roy R., *False Colors: Art, Design and Modern Camouflage*, Dysart, Iowa, 2002

Blechman, Hardy and Alex Newman, *DPM: Disruptive Pattern Material*, London, 2004

Boman, Eric and Harold Koda, *Rare Bird of Fashion: The Irreverent Iris Apfel*, London, 2007

Bonami, Francesco, Marialuisa Frisa and Stefano Tonchi, *Uniform, Order and Disorder*, Milan, 2001

Bott, Danièle, *Chanel: Collections and Creations*, London, 2007

Buttolph, Angela, *The Fashion Book*, London, 2001

Chenoune, Farid and Laziz Hamani, *Dior: 60 Years of Style: From Christian Dior to John Galliano*, London, 2007

Davies, Hywel and Nick Davies Knight, *British Fashion Designers*, London, 2008

Evans, Caroline, *Fashion at the Edge: Spectacle, Modernity and Deathliness*, New Haven, Conn., and London, 2007

Gorman, Paul, *The Look: Adventures in Rock and Pop Fashion*, London, 2006

Grand, France, *Comme des Garçons*, London, 1998

Hodge, Brooke and Patricia Mears, *Skin and Bones: Parallel Practices in Fashion and Architecture*, London, 2006

Huvenne, Paul, Emanuelle Dirix and Bruno Blonde, *Black: Masters of Black in Fashion and Costume*, Antwerp, 2010

Jackson, Lesley, *Robin and Lucienne Day: Pioneers of Modern Design*, New York and London, 2001

Jackson, Lesley, *Twentieth-Century Pattern Design*, New York and London, 2002

Jacobs, Marc, *Louis Vuitton: Art, Fashion and Architecture*, New York, 2009

Jones, Terry, *Fashion Now: Vol. 2 (Big Art)*, Cologne and London, 2008

Kirke, Charles, *Red Coat, Green Machine: Continuity in Change in the British Army 1700 to 2000*, London 2009

Koda, Harold and Kohle Yohannan, *The Model as Muse: Embodying Fashion*, New York, New Haven, Conn., and London, 2009

McDowell, Colin, *Galliano*, Rizzoli International Publications 1998

Maison Martin Margiela, *Maison Martin Margiela 20* (exhib. cat.), Antwerp, 2008

Mackrell, Alice, Richard Martin, Melanie Rickey and Suzy Menkes, *The Fashion Book*, London, 2001

Martin, Richard, *Fashion and Surrealism*, London, 1988

Mete, Fatma, 'The creative role of sources of inspiration in clothing design', *International Journal of Clothing Science and Technology*, Vol. 18, No. 4, pp.278–293 (2006)

Newark, Tim, *Camouflage*, London, 2009

Pavitt, Jane, *Fear and Fashion in the Cold War*, London, 2008

Quinn, Bradley, *The Fashion of Architecture*, Oxford, 2003

Rayner, Geoffrey, Richard Chamberlain and Annamarie Stapleton, *Artist's Textiles in Britain, 1945–1970: A Democratic Art*, Woodbridge, Suffolk, 1999

Rocha, John, *20th Century Icons: Fashion*, Absolute Press, 1999

Schiaparelli, Elsa, *Shocking Life*, London, 2007 [originally published 1954]

Sherwood, James and Tom Ford, *Savile Row: The Master Tailors of British Bespoke*, London, 2010

Smith, Paul, *You Can Find Inspiration in Everything*, London, 2003

Tucker, Andrew, *The London Fashion Book*, London, 1998

www.style.com

Barn advertising on Route 40, central Ohio. Photograph by Ben Shahn.

ACKNOWLEDGMENTS

Shelley Fox, Andrew Groves, Mark C O'Flaherty, Willie Walters, Richard Gray, David Flamee, Howard Tangye, Sharon Graubard, Elyse Heckman, Daniele Fitzgerald, Chris Moore, Holly Daws, Elinor Renfrew, Andrew Ibi, Shen Shellenberger, Fiona Grimer, Madeleine Moran, Ana Valpassos, Maria Cornejo, Max Karie, Amy Leverton, Marc Newson, Patsy Youngstein, Zaha Hadid, Davide Giordano, Helen Storey, Egle Zygas, Claire Barrett, Pip, Paul Tierney, Sue Copeland, Madelaine Kirke, Charles Kirke, Philip Marshall, Anna Sui, Chris Brooke, Bruno Basso, Nancy Chilton, Erin Yokomizo, Lynda Grose, Katy Clune, Caryn Franklin, Terry Jones, Dominique Fenn, Daniel Ezikiel Samuel the 3rd, Paul Smith, Darren Hall, Stephanie Cooper, Colette Youell, Rebecca Jarrett Amissah-Aidoo, Shelley Landale-Down, Maria Eisl, Cornelia de Uphaugh, Stephen Jones, Tony Fisher, Peter Ashworth, Derrick Santini, Kate Edmunds, Hannah Marshall. With special thanks to Emma Shackleton.

The students and staff of Parsons The New School for Design, New York, Central Saint Martins, the University of Westminster, the Royal College of Art, and Kingston University, London.

ModeMuseum, Antwerp (MOMU)
Fashion and Textiles Museum, London
Metropolitan Museum of Art, New York
Los Angeles County Museum of Art (LACMA)
Philadelphia Museum of Art
Washington Textiles Museum
Fashion and Textiles Museum, Bath
Benenden Collection, Kingston University, London

Pearly Kings and Queens – and pearly children, 1938.

Luggage porter, Waterloo Station, London, 1913.

ILLUSTRATION CREDITS

1 & 2 Imagery courtesy of Basso & Brooke
6 Repository: Library of Congress Prints and Photographs Division, Washington, D.C., 20540, USA
7 Photo by Chris Moore
8 Archive Photos/Getty Images
9 Getty Images/Hulton Archive
10 Photo by Derrick Santini
15 Photo by Topical Press Agency/Getty Images
17 Photo by Chris Moore
18–19 Images by Ronald Stoops. Courtesy MOMU Antwerp
20–23 All images by and courtesy of Paul Smith except p.21 bottom right: photo by Martin Harvey/Getty Images
24 Portrait and main image by and courtesy of Mark C. O'Flaherty
25 Left: image courtesy of www.pips-trips.co.uk; right: photo by Chris Moore
26–27 Hat photos by Peter Ashworth, courtesy Stephen Jones; p.26 left: photo

by Stephen Jones; p.27 right: photodisc/Getty Images
28–29 All images courtesy Studio M
30 Image courtesy Monica Cornejo + Zero
31 Images by Monica Feud
32–33 All images by Daniele Fitzgerald
34–35 All imagery courtesy Basso & Brooke except p.35 left: Sven Hagolani/Getty Images
36 Photo by Derrick Santini
37 Images courtesy Hannah Marshall
38–39 All images courtesy Stylesight
40 Corbis
41 Photo by Chris Moore
44 Photo by Chris Moore
45 Main image: courtesy Paul Frecker Collection; inset: courtesy Stylesight
46 Photo by Chris Moore
47 Top: Corbis; bottom: courtesy Stylesight
48 Images courtesy Stylesight
49 Collection of Anne Finch – pictures by the author

51 Left: photo by Felix Man/Getty Images; top right: courtesy Spiewak, New York; bottom right: courtesy the Benenden Collection, Kingston University, London, photo by Sean Wyatt
52 Bottom: courtesy Benenden Collection, Kingston University London, photo by Sean Wyatt
53 Getty Images
54–55 All images courtesy the Benenden Collection, Kingston University, London, photos by Sean Wyatt
56 Top: courtesy LACMA; bottom: courtesy Fashion & Textiles Museum, Bath
57 Top: courtesy Fashion & Textiles Museum, Bath; bottom left and right: LACMA
58 Images courtesy Philadelphia Museum of Art
59 Top: courtesy Washington Textiles Museum; bottom: courtesy Fashion & Textiles Museum, Bath

60 Photo by Frederik Vercruysse, image courtesy MOMU Antwerp
61 Photo by Chris Moore
62 Salvador Dalí, Fundació Gala-Salvador Dalí, DACS, 2012
63 Left: © Philadelphia Museum of Art/Corbis; right: photo by Chris Moore
64 Left: photo by Chris Moore; right: image courtesy Stylesight
65 Image courtesy Philadelphia Museum
66 Top: © ADAGP, Paris and DACS, London 2012
67 Left (two images): courtesy Stylesight; right: photo by Chris Moore
68 Bottom left: image courtesy John Lambert; bottom right: image courtesy Stylesight
69 Photo by Chris Moore
70 Left: Photo by Chris Moore; right top: image courtesy the Paul Frecker collection; right bottom: photo by Carl Mydans/Time & Life Pictures/Getty Images; centre (jacket): image courtesy Stylesight
72 Right top: Getty Images; right bottom: image courtesy Stylesight
73 Left: photo by Chris Moore; right top: photo by Daniele Fitzgerald; right bottom: image courtesy Stylesight
74 Bottom left: photo by Chris Moore; bottom right: image courtesy Stylesight; top right: courtesy the Benenden Collection, Kingston University, London, photo by Sean Wyatt
75 Joe Raedle/Getty Images
76 Top: © Jose Nicolas/Sygma/Corbis
77 Photo by Chris Moore
78 Left: image courtesy Stylesight; bottom: courtesy oldmagazinearticles.com
79 Photo by Chris Moore
80 Image courtesy Stylesight
81 Top: image courtesy Stylesight; bottom: courtesy oldmagazinearticles.com
82 Top: Portrait courtesy of Dr & Mrs Kirke; bottom: images courtesy Stylesight
83 Photo by Chris Moore
84 Getty Images Editorial
85 Right: Getty Images Editorial
86 image © Grzegorz Michalowski/PAP/Corbis
87 Top left and top right: Images courtesy Stylesight; top centre: photo by Chris Moore; bottom: Library of Congress Prints and Photographs Division, Washington, D.C., 20540, USA
88 © Peter Adams/Corbis
89 Left: photo by Chris Moore; right: courtesy Middlesex Textiles

90 Left: Getty Images; right: image courtesy the Washington Textiles Museum
91 Photos by Chris Moore
92 Top right: courtesy www.anansevillage.com; bottom: © Franck Guiziou/Hemis/Corbis collection
93 Photo by Chris Moore
94 Left and bottom: courtesy Middlesex Textiles; right: courtesy courtesy http://www.art-vs.de
95 Photo by Chris Moore
96 Top: © Lindsay Hebberd/Corbis 1988; bottom: images courtesy Stylesight
97 Photo by Chris Moore
98 Photo by Chris Moore
99 Top: © Kazuyoshi Nomachi/Corbis; bottom: images courtesy Stylesight
100 Top: © Hugh Sitton/Corbis; bottom left: Library of Congress Prints and Photographs Division, Washington, D.C., 20540, USA; bottom right: image courtesy Stylesight
101 Left: © Hugh Sitton/Corbis; right: photo by Chris Moore
102 Top: Corbis; bottom: courtesy Zaha Hadid
103 Photo by Chris Moore
106 Images courtesy of Stylesight
107 Top left: image courtesy Marc Newson; top right: Corbis; bottom: photo by Chris Moore
108 Top right: Corbis
109 Photos by Chris Moore
110 Photos by Parsha Garyesh
111 Top left: image courtesy Zaha Hadid; top right: Getty Images; bottom: LACMA Collection
112 Top: courtesy Helen Storey/Aoife Ludlow; bottom: image of Wonderland by Alex Maguire
113: Image of Wonderland by Alex Maguire
114 Library of Congress Prints and Photographs Division, Washington, D.C., 20540, USA
115 Images courtesy Stylesight
116 Images courtesy Stylesight
117 J. Bruce Baumann/ Getty Images
118 Images courtesy Stylesight
119 Library of Congress Prints and Photographs Division, Washington, D.C., 20540, USA
120 Getty Images
121 Images courtesy Stylesight
122 All images Getty Images
123 Top: Getty Images; bottom: courtesy the Benenden Collection, Kingston University, London, photo by Sean Wyatt
124 Baseball cards from Library of Congress, Benjamin K. Edwards Collection.

Library of Congress Prints and Photographs Division, Washington, D.C., 20540, USA
125 Images courtesy Stylesight
126 Bottom right: courtesy Mary Benson
127 Left: courtesy Spiewak New York; top: © Aaron McCoy/Wayne Chesledon/Getty Images
128 Photo by Chris Moore
130 Photo by Chris Moore
131 Corbis
132 Left: photo by Chris Moore; right: Corbis
133 Top: Corbis; bottom: photo by Chris Moore
134 Left: Getty Images; right: photo by Chris Moore
135 Top left: © Bettmann/Corbis; top right: photo by Chris Moore; bottom: courtesy the Benenden Collection, Kingston University, London, photo by Sean Wyatt
136 Images courtesy Darren Hall
137 Images courtesy i-D magazine/Peter Ashworth. Thanks to Terry Jones/i-D magazine
138 Images courtesy Lutz
139 Top: straight-ups courtesy Studio M; bottom: straight-ups courtesy Stylesight
140–143 All images courtesy Jens Laugesen
150 Images courtesy Shelley Fox
156 Top: images courtesy Harvey Edwards
158–159 Images courtesy Zoë Waters
160 © Bettmann/Corbis
161 Photos by Chris Moore
162 Left: photo by Chris Moore
163 Right: photo by Chris Moore
165 Left and right: photos by Chris Moore; centre: images courtesy Studio M
166 Top left and top right: photos by Chris Moore; bottom left: courtesy Paul Frecker collection; bottom right: courtesy Chicago History Museum
170 © Hulton-Deutsch Collection/Corbis
171 Top left: Time Life Pictures/Getty Images; bottom left: image courtesy Stylesight; right: photo by Chris Moore
172 Robert Llewellyn/Getty Images
173 SINEAD LYNCH/AFP/Getty Images
174 Left: © James Andanson/Apis/Sygma/Corbis; right: Getty Images
175 Top left: Guildford Borough Council Surrey UK/Getty Images; top right: photo by Chris Moore; bottom: Library of Congress Prints and Photographs Division, Washington, D.C., 20540, USA
176 Top left: courtesy Paul Frecker collection; right: Corbis; top & bottom: images courtesy Stylesight

177 Photo by Chris Moore
178 Library of Congress Prints and Photographs Division, Washington, D.C., 20540, USA
179 Left: photo by Chris Moore; centre: Getty Images; right: Buyenlarge/Time Life Pictures/Getty Images
180 © Frans Lemmens/Corbis
181 Photo by Chris Moore
182 Photo by Chris Moore
183 Left: undated photo by Nadar. BPA2# 1658 © Bettmann/Corbis; top right: MPI/Getty Images; bottom right: Corbis
184 Top left: Margaret Bourke-White/Getty Images; bottom left: © Genevieve Naylor/Corbis; right: photo by Chris Moore
185 Library of Congress Prints and Photographs Division, Washington, D.C., 20540, USA
186 Corbis
187 Photos by Chris Moore
188 Getty Images
189 Left: photo by Chris Moore; top right: hateau de Versailles, France/Getty Images; bottom right: image courtesy Chicago History Museum
190 © Lebrecht Authors/Lebrecht Music & Arts/Corbis
191 Left: photo by Chris Moore; right: Nathan Griffith/Corbis
192 © The Isamu Noguchi Foundation and Garden Museum/ARS, New York and DACS, London 2012
193 Photo by Chris Moore
194 Photo by Chris Moore
195 All images by Daniele Fitzgerald
196 Getty Images
197 © The Gallery Collection/Corbis
198 © Francis G. Mayer/Corbis
199 Photo by Chris Moore
200 Left: photo by Chris Moore; right: Courtesy Paul Frecker Collection
201 Top: JEAN-PIERRE MULLER/AFP/Getty Images; bottom: image courtesy Mark C. O'Flaherty
202 Library of Congress Prints and Photographs Division, Washington, D.C., 20540, USA
203 Reg Speller/Fox Photos/Getty Images
204 Getty Images

INDEX

Page numbers in *italic* refer to illustrations.